The Frequency, Severity, and Economic Consequences of Musculoskeletal Injuries to Firefighters in California

Seth A. Seabury, Christopher F. McLaren

Sponsored by the RAND Center for Health and Safety in the Workplace

RAND CENTER FOR HEALTH AND SAFETY IN THE WORKPLACE

A study by the RAND Institute for Civil Justice

This research was sponsored by the RAND Center for Health and Safety in the Workplace on behalf of the California Commission on Health and Safety and Workers' Compensation.

Library of Congress Cataloging-in-Publication Data

The frequency, severity, and economic consequences of musculoskeletal injuries to firefighters in California / Seth A. Seabury, Christopher F. McLaren.
p. ; cm.
Includes bibliographical references.
ISBN 978-0-8330-5002-1 (pbk. : alk. paper)
1. Fire fighters—Wounds and injuries—California. 2. Musculoskeletal system—Wounds and injuries—California. 3. Workers' compensation—California. I. McLaren, Christopher F. II. Rand Corporation. III. Title.
[DNLM: 1. Fires--California. 2. Musculoskeletal System—injuries—California. 3. Occupational Diseases—economics—California. 4. Occupational Groups—California. WE 140 S438f 2010]
RC965.F48S43 2010
617.1002'436337—dc22

2010022052

Published 2010 by the RAND Corporation
1776 Main Street, P.O. Box 2138, Santa Monica, CA 90407-2138
1200 South Hayes Street, Arlington, VA 22202-5050
4570 Fifth Avenue, Suite 600, Pittsburgh, PA 15213-2665
RAND URL: http://www.rand.org/
To order RAND documents or to obtain additional information, contact
Distribution Services: Telephone: (310) 451-7002;
Fax: (310) 451-6915; Email: order@rand.org

Preface

The past decade was a period that saw many dramatic reforms adopted and implemented in the California workers' compensation system. Many aspects of the system experienced significant overhauls, including the system for evaluating the severity of permanent disabilities, the level of benefits provided to injured workers, and the type and intensity of medical care that injured workers receive. Many of these changes have been controversial and have raised concerns that there has been an adverse impact on injured workers.

One group of injured workers with whom policymakers are particularly concerned is injured and disabled firefighters. Firefighting is dangerous, and society has a vested interest in ensuring that injured and disabled firefighters receive fair compensation and necessary medical treatment. As we discuss in this monograph, there are reasons to be concerned that different aspects of the reforms might have disproportionately affected firefighters because the nature of their jobs subjects them to a greater risk of musculoskeletal injuries. Musculoskeletal injuries are among the most common injuries in workers' compensation claims and among the most controversial. Thus, many of the reforms have provisions that affect musculoskeletal injuries, particularly back injuries, more than other kinds of injuries. If firefighters are at greater risk of incurring musculoskeletal injuries, they could have been disproportionately affected by the reforms.

This study, conducted on behalf of the California Commission on Health and Safety and Workers' Compensation, examines the frequency and severity of firefighter musculoskeletal injuries and how the reforms affected firefighters. Although our focus is on firefighters, we believe that many of the issues we study have broader implications that are relevant for all injured workers in California and, to some extent, throughout the United States.

The RAND Center for Health and Safety in the Workplace

The RAND Center for Health and Safety in the Workplace is dedicated to reducing workplace injuries and illnesses. The center provides objective, innovative, cross-cutting research to improve understanding of the complex network of issues that affect occupational safety, health, and workers' compensation. Its vision is to become the nation's leader in improving workers' health and safety policy.

The center is housed at the RAND Corporation, an international nonprofit research organization with a reputation for rigorous and objective analysis on leading policy issues. It draws on expertise in three RAND research units:

- RAND Institute for Civil Justice, a national leader in research on workers' compensation
- RAND Health, a trusted source of objective health policy research in the world
- RAND Infrastructure, Safety, and Environment, a national leader in research on occupational safety.

The center's work is supported by funds from federal, state, and private sources. For additional information about the center, please contact the director:

John Mendeloff, Director
Center for Health and Safety in the Workplace
RAND Corporation
4570 Fifth Avenue, Suite 600
Pittsburgh, PA 15213-2665
(412) 683-2300, x4532
(412) 683-2800 fax
John_Mendeloff@rand.org

Contents

Figures

Tables

Summary

Firefighting is one of the most important and most dangerous occupations in the United States. While firefighters face a number of unique risk factors in their jobs, the most common work-related injuries among firefighters are musculoskeletal disorders (MSDs). The strict physical demands of the job and limited modified work opportunities suggest that MSDs are potentially more disruptive and costly to firefighters than to people in other lines of work.

The importance of understanding the frequency and severity of firefighter MSDs has become heightened due to recent changes to the California workers' compensation landscape. Since 2004, there have been a number of changes to the workers' compensation system affecting both the level of compensation and the type and quantity of medical treatment provided to injured workers. These changes include the reduction of permanent-disability ratings that occurred due to the adoption of a new disability rating system and new rules for apportioning disability with respect to job-related causation, the adoption of treatment guidelines to provide utilization review in workers' compensation medical care, and the imposition of caps on the number of times injured workers can be reimbursed for use of chiropractic care and physical therapy. Each of these could have a potentially disadvantageous and disproportionate impact on firefighters with MSDs.

To develop a greater understanding of firefighter MSD risk and how these workers are treated by the workers' compensation system, this study pursued the following research objectives:

- Describe the average frequency and severity of work-related MSDs experienced by firefighters in California.
- Study the impact of work-related MSDs on the earnings and employment of firefighters several years after injury.
- Evaluate the impact of reforms to the disability rating system on the ratings of firefighters with permanently disabling MSDs.
- Assess whether reforms to the medical delivery system affected the employment outcomes of firefighters with MSDs.

We utilize a variety of methods and sources of data to address these questions. In this summary, we highlight our key findings.

Describing Firefighter Musculoskeletal Injury Risk

We use Bureau of Labor Statistics (BLS) injury and illness data from California for the years 2003–2007 to compare injury frequency and severity for firefighters with those of people in other occupations. Our review of these data demonstrates that firefighters face elevated risk from MSDs. Moreover, the risk is especially pronounced for firefighters 55 and older.

Specifically, we find the following:

- Firefighters are 3.5 times more likely to suffer a workplace injury and 3.8 times more likely to suffer a work-related MSD than a private-sector worker.
- Firefighters take 1.4 times longer to return to work than workers in the private sector for all injuries; this difference skyrockets for MSDs, as firefighters take twice as long to return to work.
- The median number of days away from work after an MSD is 1.8 times greater for an MSD than for any other injury for firefighters, whereas this ratio is only 1.25 for private-sector workers.
- Both the frequency and the severity of injuries, particularly MSDs, are worse for older firefighters than for younger firefighters.
- Older firefighters are 10.4 times more likely to suffer an MSD than are private-sector workers, and they take more than four times longer to return to work.

The sharp increase in the frequency of MSDs for older firefighters is consistent with the idea that the physical nature of the job exposes them to cumulative trauma, making them more susceptible to disabling MSDs at older ages. We note, however, that firefighters do receive special disability compensation and retirement benefits that could influence the reported severity and frequency of occupational injuries.

The Impact of Permanent Disabilities on the Earnings and Employment of Firefighters

The previous section indicates that firefighters, particularly older firefighters, are at greater risk of injuries, and that these injuries might be more severe in terms of their average number of lost workdays. Lost workdays represent a fairly limited measure of economic impact, however, especially in the case of permanently disabling injuries. Here, we use a large sample of permanent-disability claims for workers in California, including firefighters, to examine the earnings and employment of firefighters up to three years after an injury.[1]

When we compare across occupations, we find that the impact of a disabling injury on the employment of firefighters is similar to that of other workers in the public sector but considerably less severe than for many private-sector occupations. This finding is highlighted in Figure S.1, which reports the relative employment ratios before and after injury, by occu-

[1] We measure economic outcomes using the matching methodology developed in, among others, Peterson et al. (1998); Reville, Boden, et al. (2001); Reville, Bhattacharya, and Weinstein (2001); Reville and Schoeni (2001); Reville, Schoeni, and Martin (2002); and Reville, Seabury, et al. (2005).

Figure S.1
Relative Employment Ratios Before and After Injury, by Occupation

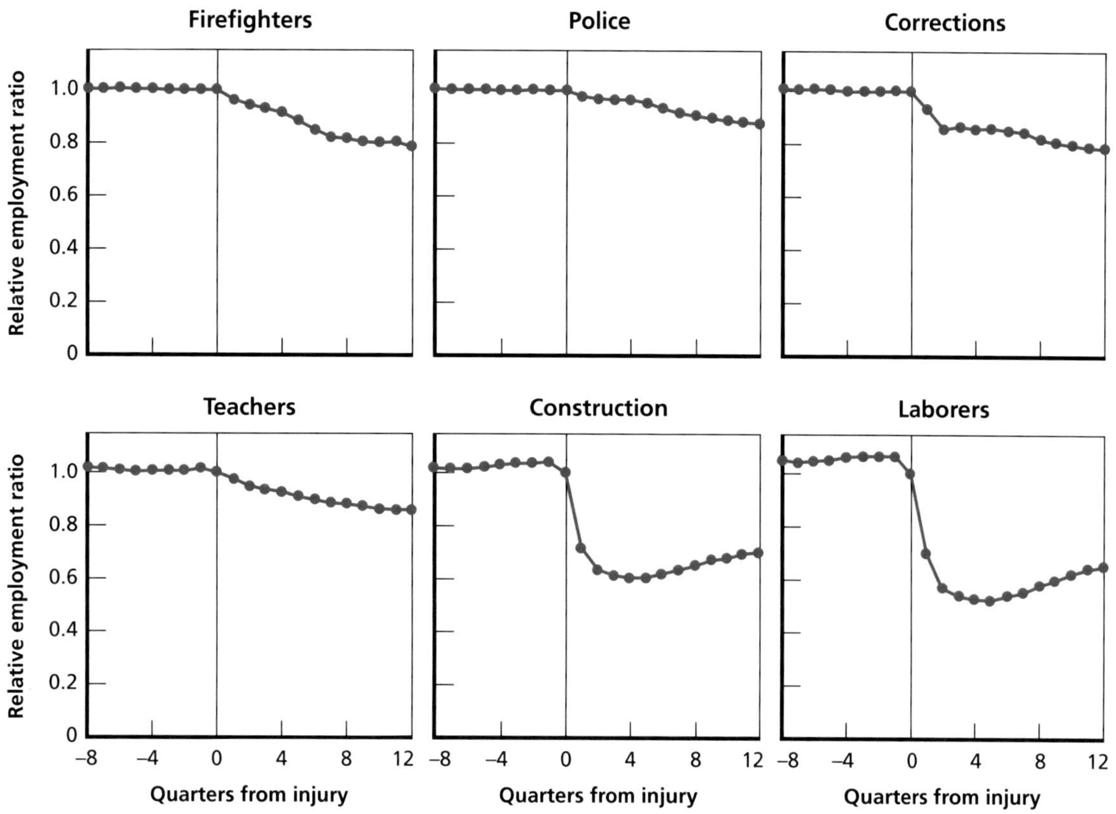

RAND *MG1018-S.1*

pation.[2] We compare firefighters to some other public safety employees (police officers and corrections officers), other public employees in a nonsafety occupation (teachers), and private-sector workers with physically demanding jobs and similar demographic profiles (construction workers and laborers). It is clear from the figure that the impact of a permanently disabling injury is considerably worse for workers in the two private-sector occupations we consider than for the public-sector workers. There is some recovery after the first six quarters after injury, but the long-term effects are extreme. As we would expect, these differences in relative employment are consistent with the differences we see in earnings losses associated with disability.

We also compare the employment outcomes of firefighters with four different categories of injuries: back injuries, knee injuries, shoulder injuries, and heart disease. We find the following:

- While the losses for firefighters who experience permanent disabilities are substantial on average, a focus on this masks considerable heterogeneity in outcomes across different injury types.

[2] The relative employment ratios are defined as the average likelihood that an injured worker is employed compared to that of the uninjured control workers. So, a relative employment ratio of 0.8 in a quarter indicates that the injured worker is, on average, 20 percent less likely to be employed in that quarter than they would have been absent the injury.

- Heart disease is associated with the most significant reduction in employment. The relative employment ratio for firefighters with heart disease falls to less than 0.6 in the third year after the date of disability.
- The losses associated with back injuries and other common types of injuries appear to be relatively minor, particularly compared to those of workers in the private sector.

While losses are relatively minor for firefighters on average, older firefighters experience more significant losses. In Figure S.2, we compare the relative employment ratios of workers with back injuries by age and occupation. Each set of bars indicates the relative employment ratios for four different age categories by occupation. In the figure, as was the case with all injuries, it is clear that the decline in employment associated with a disability for firefighters is less severe for younger workers but that, for older firefighters, it is comparable to the private-sector workers (which is not true for the other public workers).

Assessing the Impact of Reforms on Disability Ratings for Firefighters

The 2004 reforms to the California workers' compensation system were broad in scope and made many changes. Two of these changes were the introduction of a new basis for disability ratings—specifically, the American Medical Association *Guides to the Evaluation of Permanent Impairment* (AMA Guides) and new rules requiring disability ratings to be reduced to reflect apportionment with respect to causation of disability. These changes have contributed to a dramatic decline in the average disability ratings received by permanent-disability claimants in California. Because disability ratings are used to determine benefit levels, this has led to a large

Figure S.2
Relative Employment Ratios for Workers with Back Injuries Two Years After Injury, by Age and Occupation

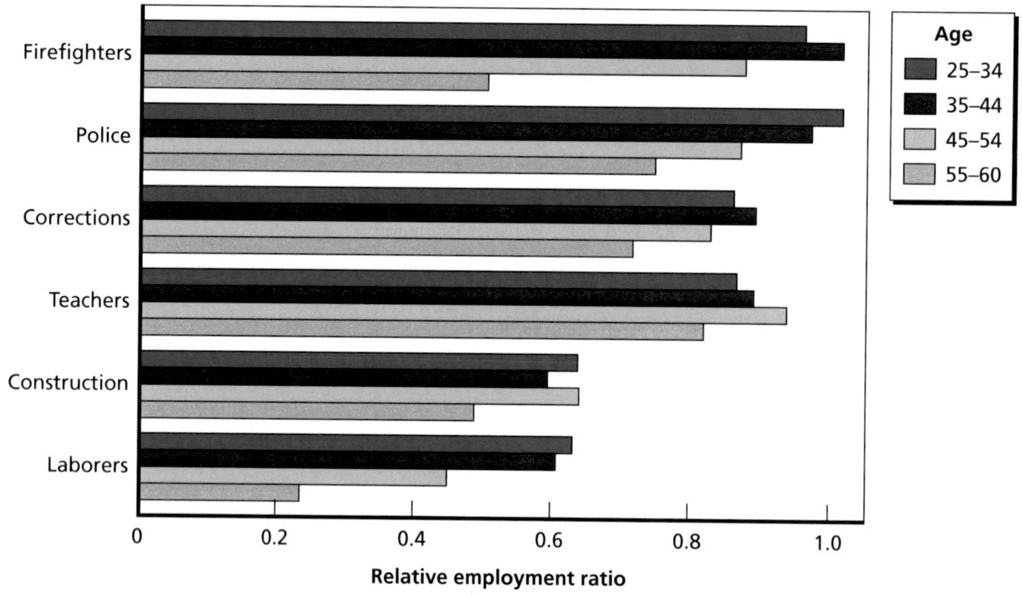

RAND *MG1018-S.2*

reduction in the average level of compensation. Our study examines how these reforms have affected the disability ratings of firefighters, particularly those with MSDs.

Figure S.3 compares the average ratings and apportionment of firefighters to those of the five other occupations considered previously for injuries occurring in 2000–2006. The figure illustrates two series. The first series reports the average ratings of claims that receive a positive rating, meaning that a physician evaluated them under the AMA Guides and found a basis for a positive rating. The second series reports the average ratings including the unrated claims as zero, meaning that no basis for a rating was found. We make this distinction because the adoption of the AMA Guides led both to a decrease in the average ratings of rated claims and to an increase in the number of claims that received no positive rating at all.

We find that firefighters experience significant declines in average ratings as a result of the new schedule being adopted. While this decline was substantial, however, it was actually somewhat less than in the other occupations. This appears to be due at least in part to the fact that the average rating for firefighters is lower than that for the other occupations in the sample. The average rating for firefighters at the end of the series appears closer to that for the other occupations. While the overall decline for firefighters is somewhat less than the other occupations, firefighters appear to have a disproportionately large fraction of cases receiving a zero rating.

Figure S.3
Trends in Permanent-Disability Ratings, by Occupation

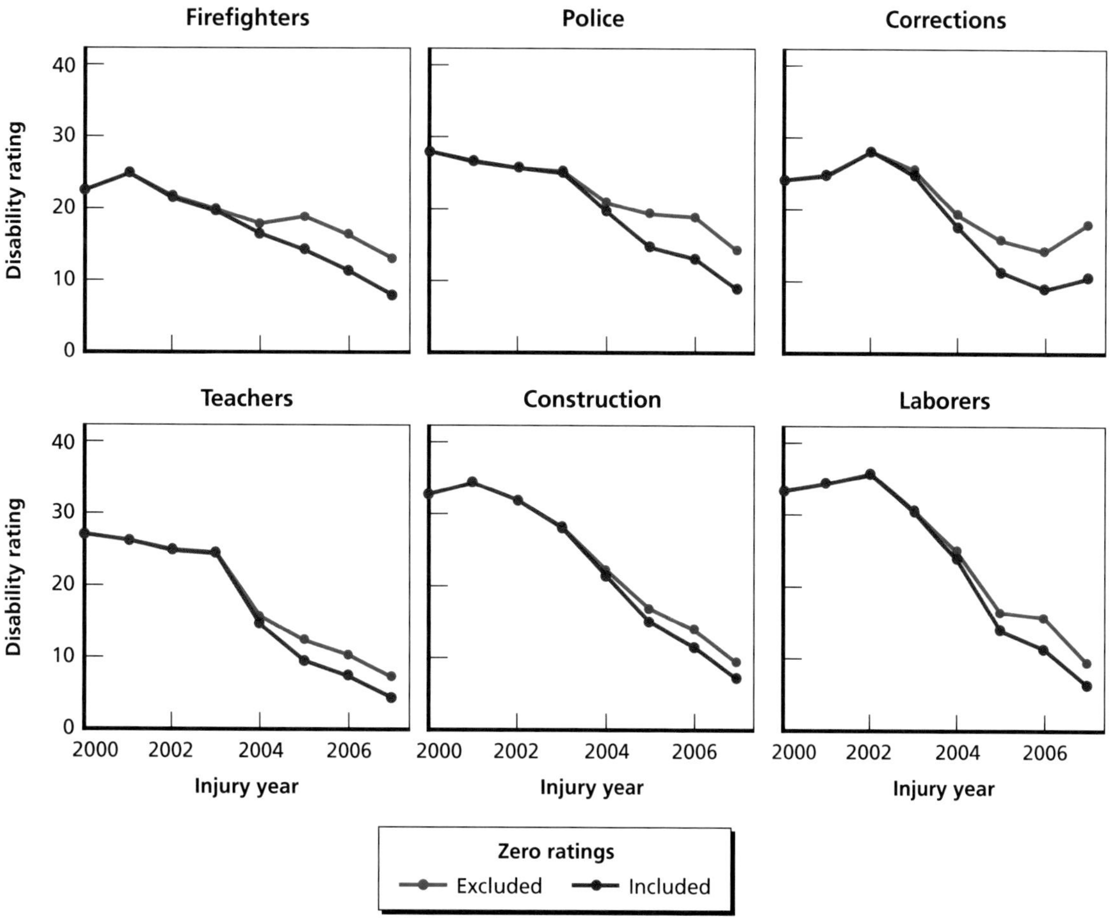

RAND *MG1018-S.3*

We also use the Disability Evaluation Unit (DEU) data to examine the impact of apportionment on the disability ratings of firefighters. We find that apportionment has led to a small reduction in the average rating for firefighters, as it has for other workers. But, while the effects are small on average, there is typically a large reduction in ratings whenever apportionment is applied.

Evaluating the Impact of Medical Reforms on Employment Outcomes for Firefighters

A number of reforms have been adopted in California affecting the medical treatment after a workplace injury. In particular, Labor Code §4604.5 imposes a limit of 24 visits to a doctor of chiropractic (DC) or physical therapist (PT) for the life of a workers' compensation claim occurring on or after January 1, 2004, unless the employer authorizes additional treatments. Furthermore, Labor Code §4610 was also adopted, requiring employers to implement utilization review systems consistent with the American College of Occupational and Environmental Medicine (ACOEM) guidelines or some other approved set of guidelines.

To evaluate the impact of the reforms, we employ a variety of methods. First, we perform a systematic literature review and analyze the Medical Expenditure Panel Survey (MEPS) to determine average utilization rates for DC and PT treatments. Next, we perform a systematic literature review to assess the existing evidence on the effectiveness of DC and PT treatments, with a focus on long-term treatments, relative to alternative methods. Finally, we conduct our own empirical analyses to evaluate whether the employment outcomes of firefighters were affected by the reforms.

Chiropractic and Physical-Therapy Utilization

Based on our utilization literature review, rates for DC and PT treatments vary by type of injury, workers' compensation status, and geographic location. Specifically, we find the following:

- Estimates from nationally representative samples of DC and PT utilization fall in the range of 10–13 visits per year.
- Median rates are significantly lower due to a small proportion of patients consuming a large majority of visits.
- Rates tend to be higher for patients with chronic low back pain and for workers' compensation claimants.
- The highest averages reported were from California workers' compensation claimants prior to the recent reforms.
- After the implementation of the cap on the number of DC and PT treatments in California, utilization rates are more comparable to national estimates.

Our analysis of MEPS yields consistent estimates with previous nationally representative samples of DC and PT utilization. Further, we find that approximately 10–15 percent of patients who go to a DC or PT at least once will exceed 24 visits. Workers' compensation claimants with an MSD who went to a physical therapist represent the highest proportion of more than 24 visits, at 15.7 percent.[3]

Existing Studies on Chiropractic and Physical-Therapy Effectiveness

Most studies evaluating the health effects of DC and PT treatments found mildly positive results relative to general practitioner (GP) care and significant improvements relative to placebos. The evidence regarding return-to-work (RTW) outcomes and cost-effectiveness was mixed and weak. While some studies do find that DC and PT treatments are marginally cost-effective and return injured workers to work faster, they are sparse, and many studies find that alternative treatments from a GP are more cost-effective. However, there is still a lack of evidence on long-term treatments.

Using our findings, we can draw some conclusions as to the overall impact of the recent cap on DC and PT treatments on firefighter outcomes:

- ACOEM guidelines suggest that virtually all injuries treated by a DC or PT injury conditions can be treated well within the new 24-treatment cap, and our utilization estimates confirm that most individuals do not exceed the caps.
- DC and PT treatment does not appear to be correlated with significantly better health, RTW, or cost-effectiveness outcomes for injured workers relative to treatment from a GP.
- While there is no evidence that the firefighters would experience differential effects of treatment, the issue has not been adequately studied.
- Firefighter DC and PT treatment levels are probably more likely to be affected by utilization review than by the cap, because utilization review is based in part on more limited ACOEM treatment guidelines.

Empirical Analysis of the Impact of the Medical Reforms

We use a statistical model that isolates the impact of the reforms from other potentially confounding factors in order to estimate whether the reforms had an impact on the employment outcomes of injured workers. Specifically, we estimate a series of multivariate regression models that estimate the likelihood that the injured worker has positive earnings in the eighth quarter after injury as a function of other characteristics of individuals. The results of our statistical analysis are reported in Table S.1.

The table provides little evidence to suggest that the reforms had a significant negative impact on employment outcomes for injured workers, and essentially no evidence of an effect on firefighters. The only coefficient that is statistically significant at conventional levels is the first estimate—the impact of the reforms on all workers for all injuries. The effect suggests a reduction of –0.03 to the relative employment ratio. The average employment level in quarter 8 of workers in our sample is 0.62, so this represents a reduction in the likelihood of working of about –4.8 percent.

It can be challenging to draw policy implications from a null result such as this. We feel that it is important to stress that our findings do not mean that the medical reforms had no effect. Rather, our findings suggest either that any effect on firefighters was too small in the average worker for us to detect or that any effect was offset by other changes in the economy

[3] The reason our MEPS estimates for PT utilization are slightly higher than for DC utilization is probably because MEPS combines PT and occupational therapy into one category.

Table S.1
Estimates from a Statistical Model of the Impact of the Medical Reforms on Employment Outcomes for Disabled Workers: Dependent Variable as Likelihood of Working Two Years After Injury

Injury	Estimated Impact of Reforms	Standard Error	p-Value
All workers			
All injuries	−0.03	0.01	0.01
Back injuries	−0.03	0.02	0.11
Shoulder injuries	−0.05	0.03	0.18
Knee injuries	−0.02	0.02	0.44
Firefighters			
All injuries	0.02	0.03	0.52
Back injuries	0.02	0.05	0.75
Shoulder injuries	0.03	0.07	0.70
Knee injuries	0.03	0.04	0.43
Heart disease	−0.15	0.20	0.46
Back injuries versus other injuries	−0.09	0.07	0.20

NOTE: The table reports the estimated effect of the medical reforms on the relative employment ratio of workers in the eighth quarter after injury. The analysis uses data on permanent-disability claims from the California Disability Evaluation Unit linked to data on earnings from the California Employment Development Department.

or the workers' compensation system. Whether the reforms had a more significant impact on workers in other occupations is unclear, though we feel that it is a subject worthy of further research.

Acknowledgments

This study has benefited considerably from the input of a number of individuals. We are grateful to the California Commission on Health and Safety and Workers' Compensation (CHSWC) for funding this research. We also wish to thank Christine Baker, the executive officer of CHSWC for her support during this project. We would also like to thank the individual commissioners and Lachlan Taylor of CHSWC for providing us with much useful input into this project. We would like to thank Ramon Cruz and Tiffany Brown from the Bureau of Labor Statistics for providing the specialized injury data we requested. Patrick Fuleihan, Santa Monica's workers' compensation administrator, was especially helpful in clarifying various aspects of the reforms. We would also like to thank Jim Hone, (now retired) chief of the Santa Monica Fire Department; Alex Rossi, chief program specialist for the County of Los Angeles; Gaynell Chase, disability benefits coordinator for the City of Oakland; and Steve Danziger, workers' compensation representative for the City of Oakland Fire Department, for their input and comments. Francis Trottier also assisted in this project.

David Powell from RAND and Surrey Walton from the University of Illinois at Chicago offered a number of helpful and insightful comments while providing technical review for the study. Finally, we would like to thank RAND colleagues Susan Gates and John Mendeloff for their comments.

Abbreviations

ACOEM	American College of Occupational and Environmental Medicine
AHRQ	Agency for Healthcare Research and Quality
BLS	Bureau of Labor Statistics
CHSWC	California Commission on Health and Safety and Workers' Compensation
CPS	Current Population Survey
DC	doctor of chiropractic
DEU	Disability Evaluation Unit
EDD	Employment Development Department
GP	general practitioner
HMO	health maintenance organization
ICD	International Classification of Diseases
ICIS	Industry Claims Information System
MEPS	Medical Expenditure Panel Survey
MSD	musculoskeletal disorder
NFPA	National Fire Protection Agency
OES	Occupational Employment Statistics
OSHA	Occupational Safety and Health Administration
PDRS	Permanent Disability Rating Schedule
PPD	permanent partial disability
PT	physical therapist
PTD	permanent total disability
QME	qualified medical evaluator
RCT	randomized control trial

RTW	return to work
TPD	temporary partial disability
TTD	temporary total disability
UCLA	University of California, Los Angeles
UI	unemployment insurance

CHAPTER ONE

Introduction

It is well understood that the provision of public safety—firefighting in particular—is one of the most dangerous occupations in the United States. Policymakers and researchers have devoted considerable attention to understanding the occupational risks firefighters face and to developing policies and equipment that help mitigate those risks. Much of this attention has focused on reducing fatal injuries. While reducing fatalities is undoubtedly an important and worthwhile policy goal, much less effort has been directed toward understanding and alleviating the risks of nonfatal occupational injuries to firefighters. In this sense, research on the occupational health and safety of firefighters has fallen considerably behind more general studies of the private sector, in which high costs of health and workers' compensation insurance have motivated employers to evaluate the effect of wellness and safety programs on costs.

Given that firefighters are, on average, several times more likely to suffer a fatal occupational injury than private workers (Clarke and Zak, 1999), it is perhaps unsurprising that so much of the research focus has been on fatal injuries. But, as we discuss in more detail later in this monograph, firefighters also face a much higher risk of suffering a nonfatal injury. If general safety improvements affected fatal and nonfatal injuries alike, this distinction would not be so important. But the nature and causes of fatal injuries are often quite different from those of nonfatal events. In particular, among the leading causes of nonfatal injury in all occupations are musculoskeletal disorders (MSDs), which have almost no bearing on fatalities.[1]

Previous studies have shown that MSDs dominate the medical costs for workers' compensation claims (Walton et al., 2003) and are the most common cause of disability retirement for professional firefighters (IAFF, 2000). There are reasons to suspect that MSDs could be more disruptive and costly to firefighters than to private-sector workers more generally. It is imperative that firefighters be in good physical condition to perform effectively and safely on a fire scene. For this reason, chronic pain or other MSDs that impair physical activity could be more disabling to firefighters than to workers in most other occupations. Furthermore, the strict physical demands of the job make it difficult to accommodate injured or disabled firefighters with modified work. The disabling effect of MSDs is probably magnified by the requirements of most firefighting positions, which generally state that workers must be fully fit for all aspects of duty and make it difficult for departments to provide modified or transitional work (see LaTourrette, Loughran, and Seabury, 2008).

---

[1] In truth, the term *musculoskeletal disorder* refers to a vast array of possible adverse health events. Generally speaking, it refers to impairment of the muscles, tendons, joints, or nerves, most commonly affecting the back or upper extremities. Later, we discuss how the specific set of injuries focused on changes depending on the nature of the data available.

The importance of understanding the frequency and severity of firefighter MSDs has become heightened due to recent changes to the California workers' compensation landscape. Since 2004, there have been a number of changes to the workers' compensation system affecting both the level of compensation and the type and quantity of medical treatment provided to injured workers. These changes include the reduction of permanent-disability ratings that occurred due to the adoption of a new disability rating system and new rules for apportioning disability with respect to job-related causation, the adoption of treatment guidelines to provide utilization review in workers' compensation medical care, and the imposition of caps on the number of times injured workers can be reimbursed for use of chiropractic care and physical therapy. Each of these could have a potentially disadvantageous and disproportionate impact on firefighters with MSDs.

To develop a greater understanding of firefighter MSD risk and how these workers are treated by the workers' compensation system, this study pursued the following research objectives:

- Describe the average frequency and severity of work-related MSDs experienced by firefighters in California.
- Study the impact of work-related MSDs on the earnings and employment of firefighters several years after injury.
- Evaluate the impact of reforms to the disability rating system on the ratings of firefighters with permanently disabling MSDs.
- Assess whether reforms to the medical delivery system affected the employment outcomes of firefighters with MSDs.

To address the first research goal, we use injury data to compare the frequency and severity of MSDs for firefighters and workers in private industry. We also match claims and earnings data to analyze return-to-work (RTW) outcomes to determine whether there are significant differences between firefighters and other workers after suffering an MSD. To evaluate the impact of the various reforms on firefighters, we use a number of different approaches. First, to determine whether firefighters have experienced the same declines in ratings as those in other occupations, we use data on disability ratings to compare the changes by occupation and type of injury. Second, to determine whether firefighters with MSDs have been hurt by new medical-treatment restrictions, we perform a systematic literature review evaluating the *expected* impact of medical reforms on outcomes, and we study trends in RTW outcomes pre and post reform.

This monograph is organized as follows. In Chapter Two, we describe frequency and severity of work-related MSDs experienced by firefighters in California. In Chapter Three, we evaluate the impact of MSDs on the earnings and employment of firefighters. In Chapter Four, we assess the impact of reforms to the rating system on firefighter disability ratings, and, in Chapter Five, we assess the impact of medical reforms on firefighter employment outcomes. The monograph concludes with a discussion of the policy implications of our findings.

CHAPTER TWO

Describing Firefighter Musculoskeletal Injury Risk

In this chapter, we use Bureau of Labor Statistics (BLS) data to analyze firefighter injury rates and median days off work for all injuries and for MSDs specifically, then compare them to those of workers in other occupations.

What Is a Musculoskeletal Disorder?

Part of the challenge in analyzing MSD risk is in correctly identifying exactly what constitutes an MSD. The term *MSD* can apply to a broad set of adverse health events that affect different parts of the body. Punnett and Wegman (2004, p. 1) define MSDs as

> a wide range of inflammatory and degenerative conditions affecting the muscles, tendons, ligaments, joints, peripheral nerves, and supporting blood vessels. These include clinical syndromes such as tendon inflammations and related conditions (tenosynovitis, epicondylitis, bursitis), nerve compression disorders (carpal tunnel syndrome, sciatica), and osteoarthrosis, as well as less well standardized conditions such as myalgia, low back pain and other regional pain syndromes not attributable to known pathology. Body regions most commonly involved are the low back, neck, shoulder, forearm, and hand. . . .

Given the diversity of injuries encompassed by the term, comparing MSD injury data from different data sources can be challenging because of the differing definitions.

For instance, the National Fire Protection Agency (NFPA) includes MSDs in a category that characterizes injuries as "strains, sprains, or muscular pain," and relevant International Classification of Diseases 9 (ICD-9) codes in the Medical Expenditure Panel Survey (MEPS) simply include diseases of the musculoskeletal system and connective tissue.[1] On the other hand, BLS has a more specific definition. The BLS definition of an MSD includes all relevant body regions and injury types, but it also specifies the event or exposure leading to the injury. Therefore, if we were to compare data from NFPA to data from BLS, we would not be making a completely accurate comparison. We would expect BLS rates to be lower than those reported by NFPA because of the more stringent definition. The availability of state-specific injury data from BLS, including MSD statistics by age, gender, and occupation, made it a convenient source of information for this study. The overall rates we discuss in this chapter might not be fully generalizable to data from other sources, though we have no reason to expect the differ-

[1] The relevant ICD-9 codes for an MSD are 710–739.

ences across groups (say, firefighters compared to other workers, or workers of different ages) to be different.

We note that, in some ways, the other main source of data we use in this monograph, data from the workers' compensation system, is particularly bad at identifying specific MSDs. The workers' compensation data we use categorize injuries chiefly by the part of the body that is disabled (e.g., back, shoulder, knee). Thus, when evaluating the MSD risk of firefighters using the workers' compensation data, we often focus simply on back injuries, the injury most commonly referred to as an MSD.

Data and Methods

We utilize an extract of BLS injury and illness data from California over the years 2003–2007. These data come from the BLS annual survey of occupational injuries and illnesses. The survey captures data from Occupational Safety and Health Administration (OSHA) employer-maintained logs of workplace injuries and illnesses. The data we use include the number of total injuries, MSDs, and related median days away from work for occupational injuries and illnesses involving firefighters, police, and the private sector. The statistics were further broken down by gender and age. In some instances, the data do not meet BLS publishable requirements due to the small populations or number of incidences (a minimum of 15 incidences in a category). Furthermore, roughly 95 percent of firefighters are male over 25 years old, so, to make more accurate comparisons across occupations, we restrict each sample to males 25 or older.[2]

Using these data, we compare average injury rates and median durations of time to return to work by occupation and injury type, as well as by age.[3] To minimize yearly sampling and reporting issues, we calculate the average injury rate as the population sample–weighted average of injury rates over the years 2003–2007. If P = total firefighter population over the years 2003–2007 and I_t = the number of injuries in year t, then the average injury rate is equal to

$$\frac{1}{P}\sum_{t=2003}^{2007} I_t.$$

We perform a similar calculation to compare relative median days off work by occupation, age, and injury type. Specifically, we compute the 2003–2007 average median as

$$\frac{1}{T}\sum_{t=2003}^{2007} I_t \times M_t,$$

[2] Unfortunately, we do not have enough observations to analyze females separately because only a small proportion of firefighters are female. However the qualitative results do not change significantly when we include females in the analysis.

[3] We used the Occupational Employment Statistics (OES) to obtain workforce populations for firefighters, police, and the private sector. Unfortunately, total employment is not broken down by age and gender for each occupation, so we used the Current Population Survey (CPS) to estimate age and gender distributions, and we applied these estimated distributions to the OES counts to obtain our workforce population sizes.

where T = total injuries for years 2003–2007, I_t = injuries in year t, and M_t is the sample-weighted median in year t.[4]

Although we obtained injury data for both local and state government workers, we combine the statistics, both to condense our findings and because most firefighters work in local government. To get a sample-weighted median combining both local and state government (the numbers are provided separately), we construct

$$M_t = \frac{L_t M_{L_t} + S_t M_{S_t}}{L_t + S_t},$$

where M_t is the averaged median for local and state government in year t, L_t and M_{L_t} are the number of local government injuries and the median days off work for local government injuries, respectively, and similarly for state government (S).

Results

Figure 2.1 compares the average injury rates for all injuries and MSDs by occupation. We compare firefighters to police officers, another public-safety occupation that is high risk and places heavy physical demands on the workforce, and workers in private industry. As we would expect, the figure shows that firefighters and police have significantly higher risks for all inju-

Figure 2.1
Average Injury Rates, by Injury Type

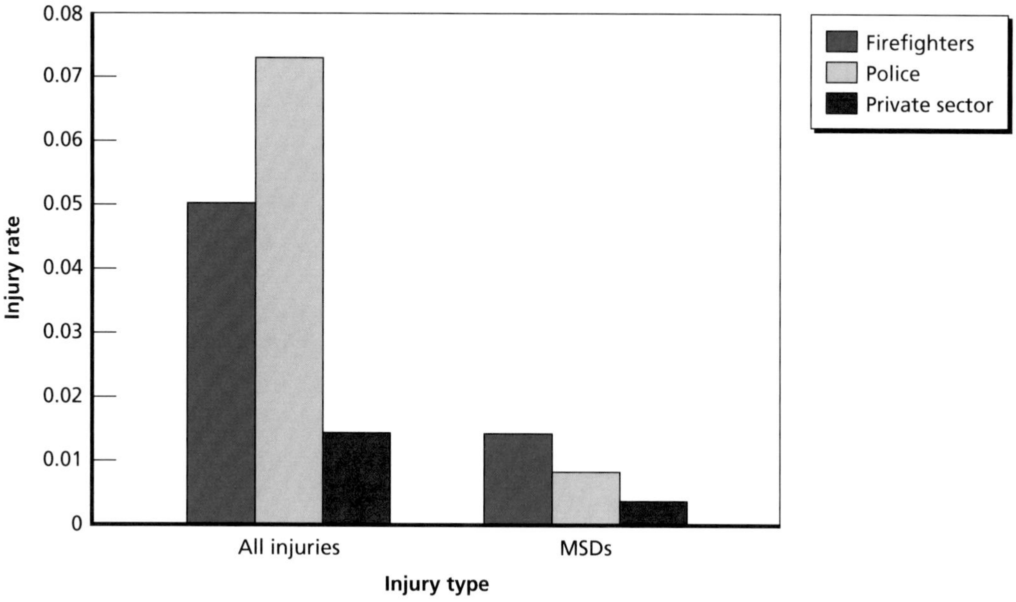

RAND *MG1018-2.1*

---

[4] BLS does not provide average days to return to work after an injury, so we are able to compare only median days off of work. We believe that averaging the sample-weighted medians over the relevant years provides a useful and robust statistic for comparing relative durations off work after an injury.

ries. Firefighters and police officers also exhibit an elevated risk of MSDs compared to workers in the private sector. The average overall injury rates are 3.5 times greater for firefighters than for workers in the private sector. This is approximately the same (3.8 times higher) if we focus on the risk of MSDs. Firefighters are slightly less likely to be injured than police officers, but they are more likely to experience an MSD.

The average injury rate provides useful information about the frequency of injuries, but we are also interested in the severity of injuries. In this chapter, we measure severity using the average number of lost workdays. Lost workdays are a natural measure of severity, because we expect that injuries that are more severe will be associated with a greater number of days away from work. If the nature of firefighting is such that it is more physically demanding and more difficult to do with a physical impairment, this should also appear in the form of increased lost workdays.

There is an important potential limitation to using lost workdays as a measure of severity across occupations, however, in that it could reflect different economic incentives. This is particularly true comparing injured workers from public-safety occupations to those in non-safety occupations. As we discuss in more detail in Chapter Three, injured police officers and firefighters in California (and most other states) receive extra injury and disability compensation compared to workers injured in the private sector. The additional injury compensation could give workers more incentive to remain out of work after an injury (see Meyer, Viscusi and Durbin, 1995). Additionally, older firefighters receive disability retirement benefits that are generous compared to those of private-sector workers, which could affect their incentives to report or remain out of work after an injury when close to retirement age.[5] Thus, any differences we observe in injury durations across occupations should be interpreted with this potential incentive effect in mind. We do note, however, that these different compensation packages are in place for all injuries. This means that, when we compare differences between MSDs and other injury types for firefighters to those for private-sector workers, the differences will not necessarily be driven by different compensation packages.

Figure 2.2 compares occupational differences in the median number of days off work for all injuries and for MSDs. The median number of days off work for firefighters for any type of injury is about 17 days, whereas, for an MSD, the median is about 30 days—about 1.8 times higher. For workers in the private sector, the median number of days off work for any type of injury is 12 days. The median number of days off work after an MSD is 15 days, about 1.25 times higher. Comparing medians for firefighters with those of private-sector workers, we see that firefighters remain out of work longer after any injury. But that difference skyrockets for MSDs, because firefighters take twice as long to return to work. This is at least consistent with the belief that MSDs are particularly harmful to firefighters because of the strenuous physical demands of the job and limited modified-work opportunities. The injury durations for firefighters are roughly comparable to those for police, in terms of all injuries and MSDs.

One of the defining characteristics of MSDs is that they are commonly associated with cumulative factors, so they develop and worsen over time. Given the physically demanding nature of firefighting, it is natural to suppose that firefighters might be more subject to cumulative trauma that ultimately leads to physical impairment. To explore this, we examine the injury rates—MSD and otherwise—of firefighters in different age ranges. If firefighters are

---

[5] See LaTourrette, Loughran, and Seabury (2008) for a summary of the disability retirement benefits provided to public-safety employees.

Figure 2.2
Median Days Off Work, by Injury Type

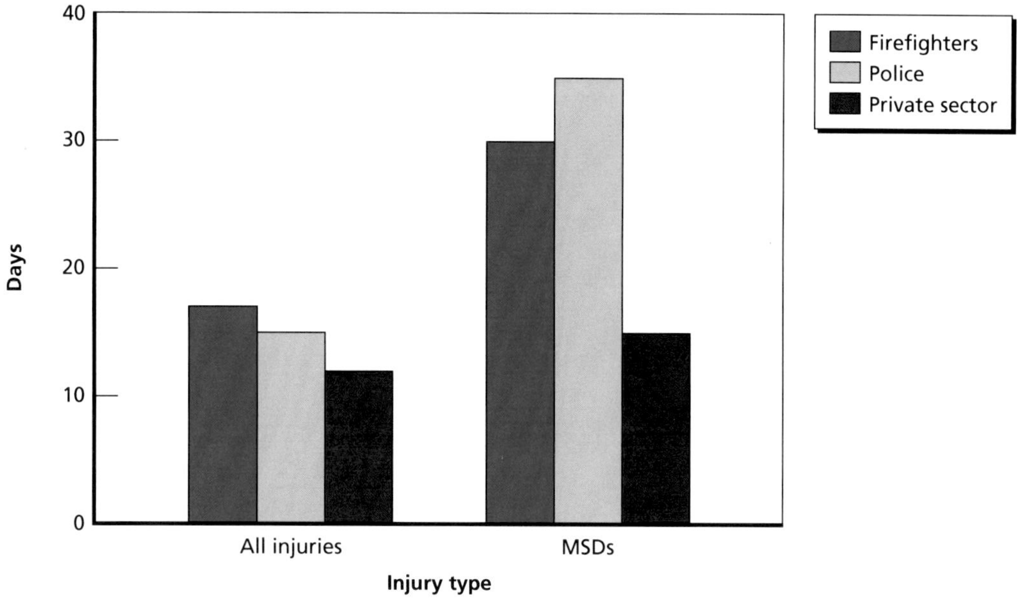

RAND *MG1018-2.2*

exposed to greater amounts of cumulative trauma, we would expect to see a higher rate of MSD injuries for older firefighters.

In our private-sector data, the expected relationship between age and injury risk is somewhat ambiguous. Older workers in physically demanding private-sector jobs could also be more subject to cumulative trauma. On the other hand, because we look at a cross-section of workers in different occupations, it is possible that the older workers in our sample have different jobs that are associated with less risk or are less physically demanding, potentially offsetting these risk factors. More generally, the relationship between age and injury risk is not well understood (Chau et al., 2010).

Figure 2.3 compares the average injury rates for male firefighters and private-sector workers by age.[6] Interestingly, the figure suggests no clear differences in injury rates for private-sector workers by age. Younger workers have the highest injury rate, at almost 2 percent, but the overall difference across age categories is small. This could reflect differences in occupation to which we alluded before, with older workers taking jobs associated with less injury risk. While there is little difference across age categories for private-sector workers, there is a clear pattern of increasing injury rates for older firefighters. Firefighters over the age of 55 have an injury rate that is 3 percentage points greater than firefighters under the age of 45 years (more than a 60-percent increase in risk).

Figure 2.4 compares the MSD injury rates of firefighter to those of private-sector workers by age. As was the case with all injuries, there is little difference in the MSD injury rate across age categories for private-sector workers, though older workers do appear to have slightly lower injury rates. In general, there appears to be a slight positive correlation between firefighter MSD injury rates and age for workers under 55 years of age. Firefighters 55 years and older,

---

[6] We do not include police officers in this analysis because the data on police were not reported in sufficient detail to allow us to provide age breakdowns.

Figure 2.3
Average Injury Rates, by Age

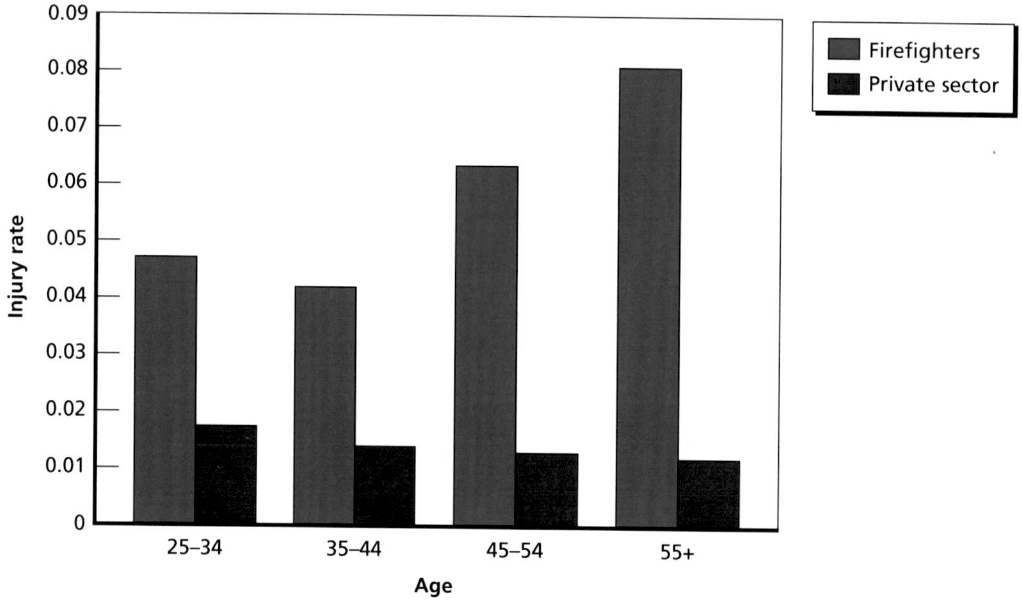

RAND *MG1018-2.3*

Figure 2.4
Average Musculoskeletal-Disorder Injury Rates, by Age

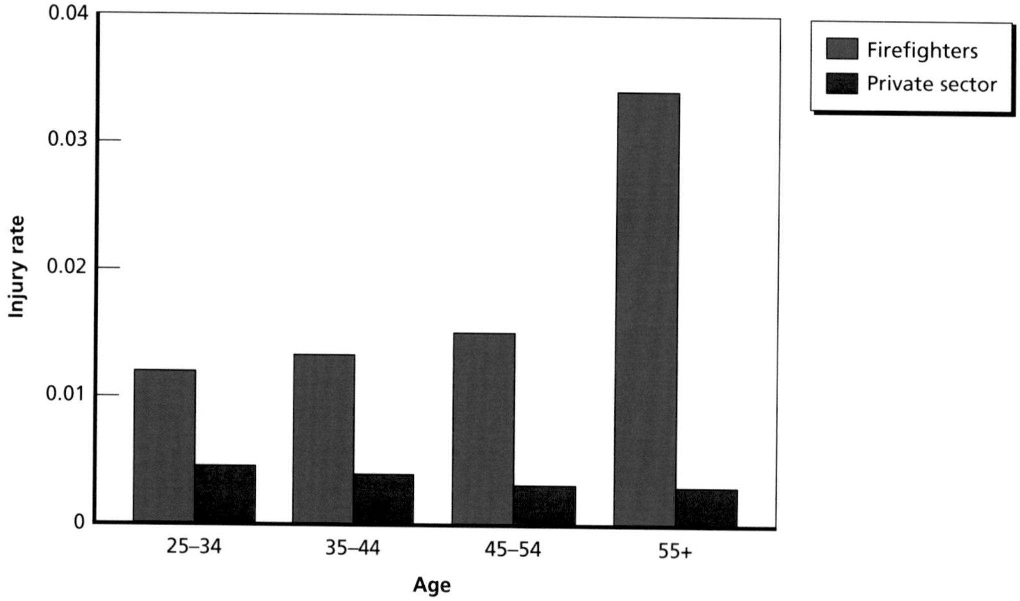

RAND *MG1018-2.4*

however, have an MSD injury rate that is more than double that of the youngest firefighters and more than ten times greater than that of private-sector workers of the same age. Comparing Figures 2.3 and 2.4, it is apparent that older firefighters are associated with much higher rates of reported workplace injuries than both younger firefighters and private-sector workers.

Moreover, this difference is more pronounced for MSDs than it is for all injuries combined. This is consistent with the notion that the rigorous physical demands of firefighting subject them to trauma throughout their working lives, making them more subject to MSDs in later years.

We also examine how injury durations relate to age. Figure 2.5 reports the median number of days off work after any lost-workday injury for firefighters and private-sector workers by age. Unlike in the analysis of injury rates, there does appear to be an increase in injury duration for older private-sector workers. Thus, while injuries appear to be somewhat less common for older private-sector workers, it appears to take them longer to recover when an injury does occur. The relationship is even more pronounced for firefighters. The figure shows that firefighters have greater median durations of time to return to work for each age group; moreover, the difference increases with age. The median number of days away from work for firefighters age 55 and older is more than ten days higher than that for private-sector workers in the same age category.

The differences in injury duration by age are even more pronounced when we restrict the injury sample to MSDs. Figure 2.6 compares the median number of days away from work for firefighters and private-sector workers with MSDs by age. While it is difficult to tell because of the scale being different from that in Figure 2.5, the median number of days away from work is higher for every age category in both occupations for MSDs than for all injuries. As before, the median days away from work is also generally increasing in age for both occupations. What is most striking about the figure, however, is that the median number of days away from work for firefighters age 55 and over is so much higher than for any other group. The median number of days away from work for the oldest firefighters is more than 90, which is several times higher than that of the next-oldest group of firefighters or the oldest private-sector workers.

Figure 2.5
Median Days Off Work, by Age, for All Injuries

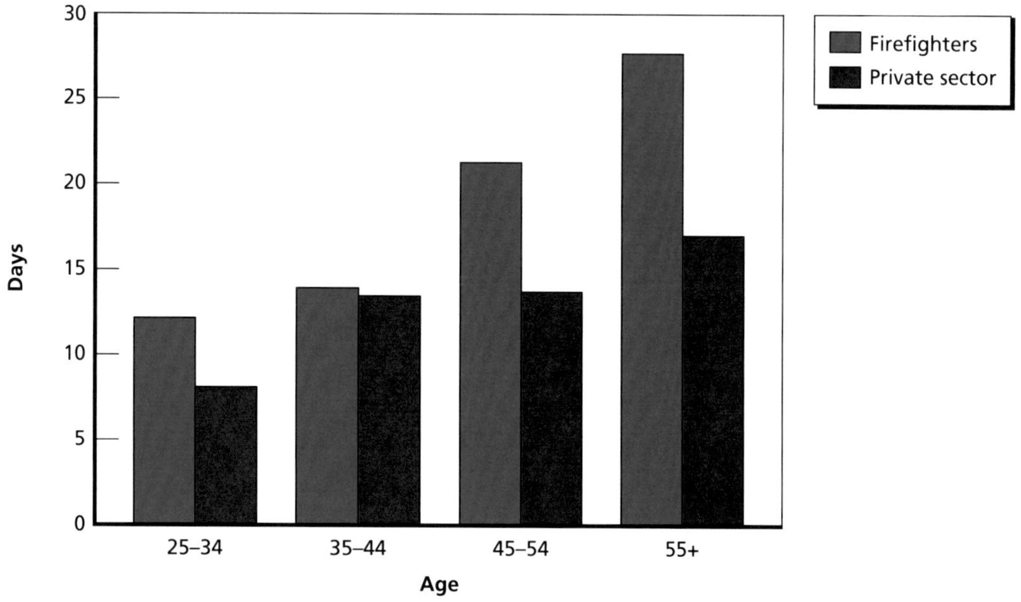

RAND *MG1018-2.5*

Figure 2.6
Median Days Off Work, by Age, for a Musculoskeletal Disorder

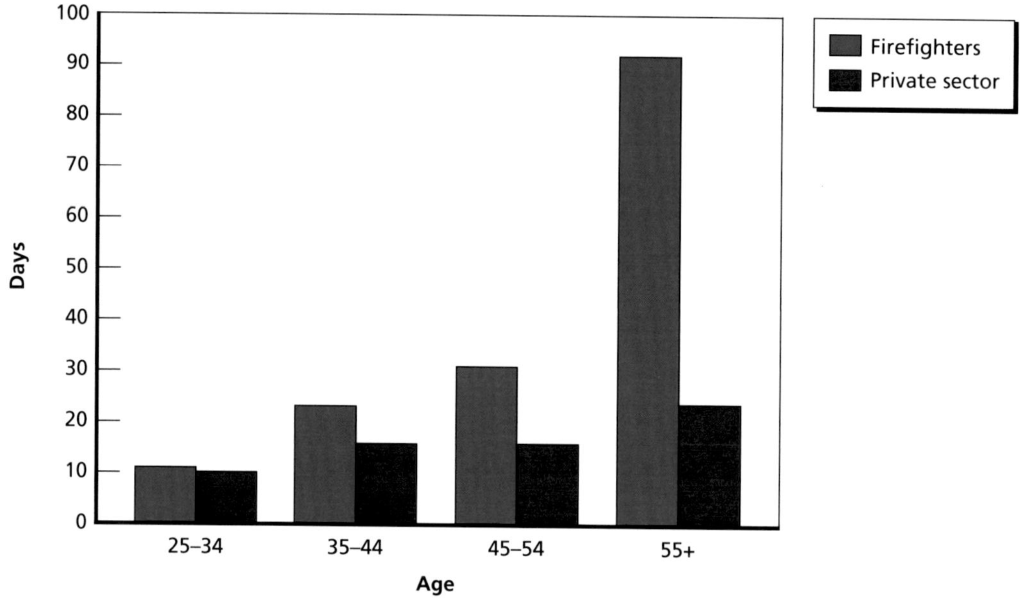

RAND *MG1018-2.6*

While the impact of MSDs on firefighters is most pronounced for the oldest workers, MSDs represent a comparatively small fraction of the sample of injuries. Figure 2.7 reports the fraction of total MSD injuries that are accounted for by each age category of worker.[7] The proportion of MSD injuries is highest for both the firefighters and private-sector workers for the 35- to 44-year-olds. But the oldest workers, those 55 and over, account for only about 12 percent of all MSD injuries for firefighters or for private-sector workers. The fraction of firefighters 55 or older represents a considerably smaller portion than for private-sector workers, so older firefighters do represent a disproportionately high fraction of injuries.[8] Nevertheless, we do note that the overall share of total injuries is relatively small.

Summary

Based on our review of BLS injury data, it is clear that firefighters are at greater risk of being injured on the job than are other workers and that the risk is particularly higher for MSDs. Specifically, we found that firefighters are 3.5 times more likely to suffer a workplace injury and 3.8 times more likely to suffer a work-related MSD. Firefighters also take a significantly longer amount of time to return to work, particularly after an MSD. We found that median durations of time away from work after an injury are higher for firefighters than for private-sector workers. Additionally, the median number of days away from work after an MSD is 1.8 times greater for an MSD than it is for all injuries combined for firefighters, whereas this ratio is only 1.25 for private-sector workers.

---

[7] The proportion of injuries by age is roughly the same when we look at all injuries.

[8] Our estimates from the CPS suggest that just 5 percent of firefighters in California are age 55 or over, compared to 15 percent of all private-sector workers in California.

Figure 2.7
Proportion of Musculoskeletal Disorders, by Age

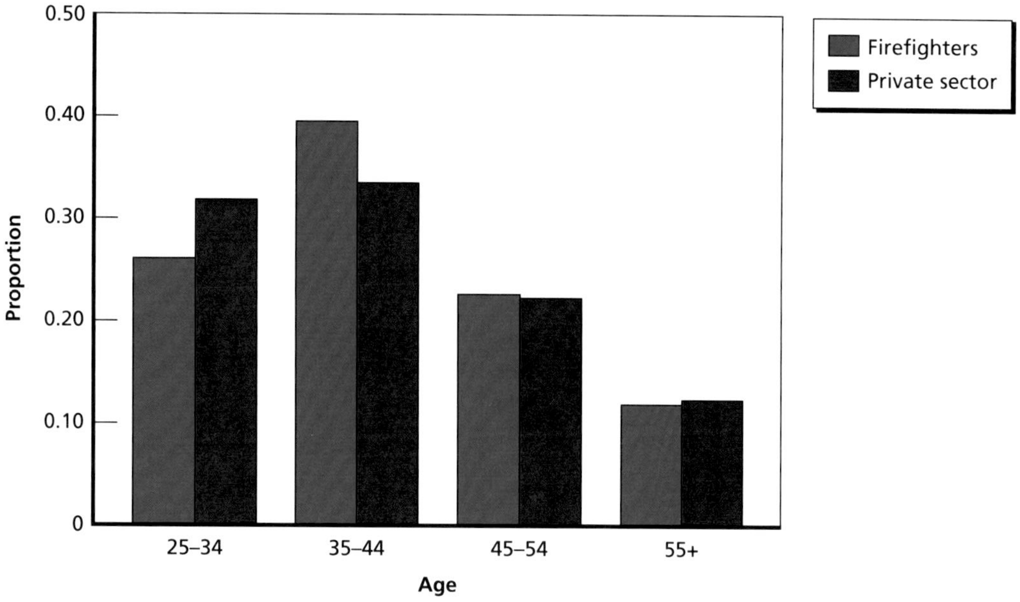

RAND *MG1018-2.7*

We also find that both the frequency and the severity of injuries, particularly MSDs, are worse for older firefighters than for younger firefighters. While severity is also worse for workers in the private sector, the frequency is generally lower. We find that older firefighters are 10.4 times more likely to suffer an MSD than are private-sector workers and that they take more than four times longer to return to work. This finding is consistent with the idea that firefighters experience greater cumulative trauma that makes them more susceptible to injury and disability at older ages. It is important to note, however, that we cannot rule out the possibility that these difference are due at least in part to the additional disability compensation and retirement benefits provided to firefighters.

This chapter has demonstrated that firefighters have significantly higher risks and longer durations of time out of work after an injury, particularly for an MSD. In the next chapter, we take a deeper look into this problem by evaluating the earnings and employment consequences of permanent disabilities to firefighters.

CHAPTER THREE

Evaluating the Impact of Permanent Disabilities on the Earnings and Employment of Firefighters

In this chapter, we examine the impact of permanently disabling workplace injuries—in particular, MSDs—on the long-term earnings and employment of firefighters. The previous chapter indicates that firefighters, particularly older firefighters, are at greater risk of injuries than are people in the private sector and that these injuries might be more severe than other types of injuries in terms of their average number of lost workdays. Lost workdays represent a fairly limited measure of economic impact, however, especially in the case of permanently disabling injuries. Here, we use a large sample of permanent-disability claims for workers in California, including firefighters, to examine the earnings and employment of firefighters up to three years after an injury.

Injury Compensation for Firefighters in California

While firefighters face a greater risk of injury, they also receive special compensation measures that are unavailable to most private-sector workers. These include enhanced injury benefits and disability retirement options that could help offset any differences in risk or economic outcomes. Here, we offer a brief summary of the differences in benefits received by firefighters in California. For a more detailed description see LaTourrette, Loughran, and Seabury (2008).

Most individuals who suffer an occupational injury or illness in the United States receive compensation from their employer as mandated by the workers' compensation system in force in their state. Workers' compensation requires employers to pay medical and indemnity benefits to injured workers. Typically, workers receive full (or mostly full) coverage for all medical expenses and receive compensation for some fraction of lost wages. The indemnity benefits vary depending on whether the injury is permanent or temporary. Generally, there are five types of indemnity benefits: temporary total disability (TTD) benefits, permanent partial disability (PPD) benefits, permanent total disability (PTD) benefits, temporary partial disability (TPD) benefits, and fatality benefits.

The indemnity benefits offered to public employees are often more generous than those offered to private employees, and this is particularly true for public-safety employees. Most state workers' compensation programs provide weekly TTD benefits that are equal to two-thirds of preinjury weekly earnings, subject to a cap (e.g., two-thirds of weekly wages up to $500 per week). Workers' compensation benefits are tax free at the state and local levels, though some states (e.g., Ohio) set benefits as a fixed fraction of after-tax earnings.

Many public employees receive negotiated benefits called *salary continuance*, which replaces a portion of wages that is higher than the standard two-thirds of preinjury weekly earnings for some limited period of time after an injury. There is no set formula for salary continuance, but a common example would be a worker receiving 80 percent of preinjury salary for the duration of his or her injury. In principle, salary continuance can be negotiated for private employees as well, though anecdote suggests that it is far more common for public employees (perhaps due to the higher rates of unionization among public employees).

Public-safety employees are sometimes given higher temporary benefits as a result of legislative action. In California, Labor Code §4850 provides police officers, firefighters, and other designated public-safety employees with their full salary, tax free, for up to one year following a work-related injury. Public-safety employees are not necessarily the only public workers offered special benefits. While less generous, public-school teachers in California are also granted special benefits; Section 44984 of the Education Code requires that any certificated employee injured at work be given his or her full salary, tax free, for 60 workdays (Education Code §44984[d]).[1]

Another key difference in the compensation for public-safety employees is the coverage offered for certain chronic illnesses that is not offered to workers in the private sector. Most workers have to prove that an illness is job related in order to receive compensation. In the case of public-safety employees, certain diseases are presumed to be work related. These include heart disease, respiratory disease, and certain types of cancer. These presumptions are offered because there is concern that public-safety employees are routinely exposed to risk factors during their employment that put them at greater risk of these conditions, although, as LaTourrette, Loughran, and Seabury (2008) notes, these presumptions have not been scientifically validated. California has presumptions in place for all three of these health conditions for both police officers and firefighters. As a result, we observe workers' compensation claims for certain conditions, predominantly heart and lung disease, which we do not observe for workers in other occupations.

Data and Methods

We measure economic outcomes using the matching methodology developed in, among others, Peterson et al. (1998); Reville et al. (2001, 2002); Reville, Bhattacharya, and Weinstein (2001); Reville and Schoeni (2001); and Reville, Seabury, et al. (2005).

Measuring Losses from Injury

We describe the empirical challenge to estimating earnings losses using Figure 3.1, which illustrates the hypothetical losses from a permanently disabling workplace injury. The dashed line represents the potential earnings a worker would have in the absence of an injury. Potential earnings increase over time, representing the increased earnings associated with increasing experience in the labor market or increasing tenure with the employer. The solid line represents the actual earnings of the injured worker. At the time of injury, the worker receives no earnings for some time while recovering from the injury. This is the period during which workers' compensation temporary disability benefits are received or, in the case of firefighters, some

[1] The term *certificated employee* refers to someone employed in a position that requires a certificate of qualifications but who is not necessarily a teacher (Education Code §1294).

Figure 3.1
Hypothetical Effect on Earnings After a Workplace Injury

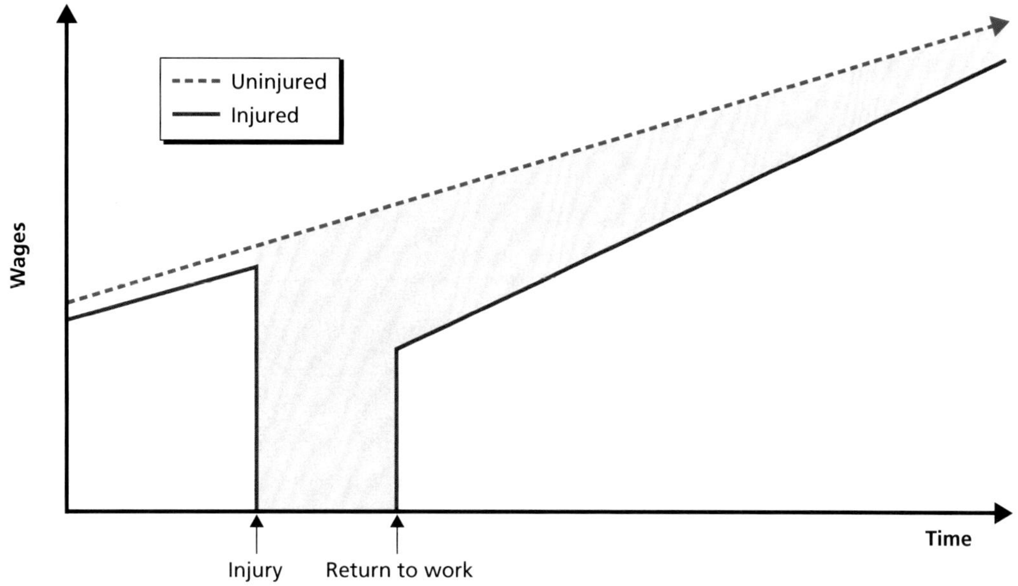

RAND *MG1018-3.1*

combination of salary continuance, temporary disability benefits, and Labor Code §4850 benefits are earned.

At some point, the worker returns to work, perhaps in some modified capacity. In the example in the figure, the worker returns at earnings lower than she was earning prior to injury. The worker recovers earnings over time, as the wages converge closer to what they would have been absent the injury. In this example, at the end of the observed period, the worker makes more than she made prior to the injury but not as much as she would have made if she had not been injured.

The shaded area in the figure represents the total lost earnings over the period after the injury. Estimating the size of this area and determining what fraction is replaced by workers' compensation benefits are the goals of this analysis. Whereas wages received while the claimant is injured are readily observable (the solid line in Figure 3.1), the challenge in estimating earning losses lies in estimating the uninjured earnings, which are represented by the dotted line.

This example illustrates the metrics we can use to estimate the economic impact of a disability. The shaded area in Figure 3.1 represents the total earnings lost as a result of the disability. To measure the length of time out of work, we can measure whether the employee has returned at different points after injury (i.e., measuring the point of return to work). Whether we evaluate the impact on the actual dollars earned or the time out of work, both represent adverse outcomes for injured workers.

Using Matched Uninjured Coworkers as a Control Group

We estimate uninjured earnings in the postinjury period using the earnings of a matched comparison (control) group. This approach draws its inspiration from the training program evaluation literature (see Heckman and Hotz, 1989; Holland, 1986; and LaLonde, 1986). The control group is made up of workers similar to the injured workers in the preinjury period but who did not experience a workplace injury during the time period under examination.

For the comparison group, we selected up to five workers at the same firm who had earnings close to the injured worker's over the year prior to injury. The comparison workers were also required to have similar tenure, where tenure is measured using three levels: less than or equal to one year on the job, one to two years, or more than two years. In each quarter after injury, we calculated the difference between the injured worker's earnings and the average earnings of the worker's comparison group. This gave us the estimate of earnings loss in that quarter. We repeated this calculation for quarters prior to the injury as well, in order to test the quality of the match. We describe this approach formally in the next paragraphs.

Let y_t^I represent the injured worker's earnings (where *I* denotes "injured" and the subscript *t* denotes time from the injury). Let y_t^U represent the comparison worker's earnings (where *U* denotes "uninjured"). We estimated y_t^U using the average earnings of the *n* comparison workers for that individual injured worker, where *n* is between 1 and 5, depending on the number of available comparable uninjured workers at the injured worker's employer. For any injured worker, the undiscounted earnings loss between the time of injury, which we denoted as $t = 0$, and some future date, *T*, is shown in Equation 3.1.

$$\text{earnings loss} = \sum_{t=0}^{T} \left(y_t^U - y_t^I \right). \quad (3.1)$$

Usually, when we report earnings losses, we report the average of the quantity in Equation 3.1 across all injured workers. In many cases, we were interested in estimating proportional earnings losses, or that fraction of potential uninjured earnings over a period of time that an injured worker loses. Normalizing earnings losses by what the individual would have made facilitates comparison over time when average earnings might be growing. It also allows comparison across firms that have different average earnings, such as different industries or different states. Proportional earnings losses are estimated as earnings losses divided by the total earnings received by the comparison group, as shown in Equation 3.2.

$$\text{proportional earnings loss} = \frac{\sum_{t=0}^{T} \left(y_t^U - y_t^I \right)}{\sum_{t=0}^{T} y_t^U}. \quad (3.2)$$

Note that, while we describe the earnings loss here without discounting, we actually compute earnings losses using quarterly discounting as described in Reville et al. (2001).

In some sense, RTW is easy to measure: We simply observe whether or not an individual is working (and at what point) after an injury occurs. In some cases, however, injured workers might exit the labor force for reasons totally independent of their disability. Simply asking whether disabled workers are working in the postinjury period ignores the possibility that they might not have worked even in the absence of a disability. Thus, to estimate the impact of injuries on RTW, it is necessary to compare the likelihood that disabled workers are working in the postinjury period with the likelihood that uninjured control workers are working.

We can formally define our RTW estimates as follows. Let h_t^I be a variable that equals 1 if earnings are reported by an injured worker in quarter t (i.e., if $y_t^I > 0$), and let h_t^U be a similar indicator for uninjured workers (we focus on quarters because the data we propose to use are quarterly earnings data). If a person has earnings reported in that quarter, then we presume that they are working in that quarter. Furthermore, let $\Pr\left(h_t^I\right)$ and $\Pr\left(h_t^U\right)$ denote the probability that injured and uninjured workers report positive earnings in quarter t. In general, we do not observe the probability that an individual works—we simply observe whether the individual works. However, aggregating into the fraction of individuals who work provides us with an estimate of the probability that an individual works. We can thus define RTW in a given quarter as

$$\text{relative employment}_t = \frac{\Pr\left(h_t^I\right)}{\Pr\left(h_t^U\right)}. \qquad 3.3$$

In some cases, we might ask whether an individual returns to the same employer for which he or she worked at the time of injury, or the *at-injury employer.* Return to the at-injury employer can be examined in a similar fashion, with the h_t variables equaling 1 only if the injured worker reports earnings from the at-injury employer.

Linked Administrative Data

Our data in this study are similar to the data used in past studies, (e.g., Peterson et al., 1998; Reville, Seabury, et al., 2005). Workers' compensation claim data are linked to earnings data for the claimant based on his or her Social Security Number, and this information is combined with earnings data to identify the control group. We use data on ratings from the California Disability Evaluation Unit (DEU).

The DEU performs between 60,000 and 80,000 ratings of permanent disabilities each year. The data set used here was drawn from evaluations done on injuries occurring between 2000 and 2007. The DEU data contain specific information about the type of impairment, severity of the impairment, and important demographic data (including age at injury and occupation).

The earnings data are from the base-wage file maintained by the California Employment Development Department (EDD). Every quarter, employers covered by unemployment insurance (UI) in California are required to report the quarterly earnings of every employee to the EDD. These reports are stored in the base-wage file. The industries covered by UI are virtually identical to the industries covered by workers' compensation, so a worker injured at a firm for which he or she can make a workers' compensation claim should also have a record for that quarter in the base-wage file. With roughly 95 percent of employees in California covered by the UI system, the matched DEU-EDD data provide a substantially complete and accurate California quarterly earnings history for permanent-disability claimants. We have all the available data for every worker from the first quarter of 1998 through the fourth quarter of 2009.[2]

[2] Data are not available in every year for every worker whom we observe at the time of injury. In some cases, injured or comparison workers drop out of the sample and we do not know whether they left the state, stopped working, or are missing for some other reason. This issue is discussed in greater detail in Reville and Schoeni (2001).

There is no uniform coding scheme for occupation in the DEU data; rather, occupation is identified by a text field. We created an occupation code using a search algorithm that identified specific string patterns. For example, to identify firefighters, we identified workers with the term "fire" in the occupation field, then eliminated candidates that were obviously not in the fire service (e.g., claims for which the occupation field included such terms as "sprinkler," "installer," or "apparatus"). Using this technique, we identified 4,951 permanent-disability claims filed by firefighters from 2000 to 2007.

We used the same technique to identify several other occupations to compare to firefighters. To compare to other public-safety occupations, we identified police officers and Department of Corrections employees (including parole officers). We identified teachers, giving us another occupation that is made up largely of unionized workers with public employers but one that is not a public-safety occupation. Finally, we selected two private-sector jobs—construction and laborers—that are more comparable to firefighting. That is, both are physical occupations whose workers are more likely to be male, though likely without the training, union status, or job security that most firefighters possess. Including firefighters, we included 49,167 claims across these six occupations in our analysis.

There is an important limitation to examining occupation-specific earnings and employment outcomes. Specifically, the occupation field comes from the DEU, and we do not have the comparable information on the occupations of uninjured workers. That is, we match workers only by employer and preinjury earnings, so it is possible that we match injured firefighters to uninjured workers who are not firefighters.

Results

We begin by summarizing the distribution of injury types in the DEU data by occupation, reported in Table 3.1. The table reports the 21 categories of disability used by Reville, Seabury, et al. (2005), which combines cases with multiple types of disabilities as a single, separate category. Each cell reports the percentage of all permanent-disability claims in a given occupation that are attributable to that injury category (i.e., the columns sum to 100, barring rounding error).

The table indicates several differences in the injury risks for firefighters compared to the other occupations. First, even though we know from the previous chapter that firefighters face higher MSD risk, the percentage of back injuries is actually about average in this sample. A higher percentage of firefighter claims are back injuries than is the case with police or corrections, but the percentage is lower than for construction workers or laborers. Second, firefighters appear more likely to experience shoulder or knee injuries than any of the other occupations. Hearing loss also appears to be a more common injury claim for firefighters than for other occupations. A lower fraction of firefighter injuries involve multiple types of injuries than is true for any other occupation.

The table also confirms the higher fraction of chronic-disease cases that are considered job related for public-safety employees, at least in the case of heart disease. Approximately 2.6 percent of claims for firefighters involve heart disease, while 4.3 percent of police officer claims and 3.8 percent of corrections claims are for heart disease. The percentage of claims involving heart disease in the other occupations is minuscule.

Table 3.1
Distribution of Injury Types in the Disability Evaluation Unit Data, by Occupation

	Percentage of All Permanent-Disability Claims						
Injury	**Firefighters**	**Police Officers**	**Corrections**	**Teachers**	**Construction**	**Laborers**	**All**
Back (including neck)	23.8	20.4	19.6	23.9	24.4	26.5	23.5
Shoulder	10.3	7.9	7.7	7.9	6.7	5.4	7.3
Elbow	1.7	1.5	1.2	1.5	2.2	1.4	1.7
Wrist	0.6	1.0	0.6	1.2	1.1	0.8	1.0
Hand or fingers	1.7	2.2	1.7	2.3	5.6	4.7	3.6
Other upper extremity	2.7	4.6	4.9	5.8	7.0	6.6	5.7
Loss of grasping power	2.2	3.5	3.9	4.1	5.5	6.0	4.5
Hip	0.4	0.2	0.1	0.3	0.1	0.1	0.2
Knee	18.6	14.3	16.3	16.2	10.1	6.9	12.6
Ankle	4.7	4.0	4.1	5.3	3.7	3.5	4.1
Toe(s)	0.1	0.1	0.2	0.1	0.1	0.1	0.1
General lower extremity	1.56	1.55	2.39	2.24	2.02	1.61	1.87
Heart disease	2.6	4.3	3.8	0.2	0.1	0.1	1.4
Chronic lung	0.6	0.2	0.4	0.3	0.2	0.1	0.3
Vision	0.1	0.2	0.0	0.1	0.6	0.8	0.4
Hearing	4.0	3.1	0.5	0.3	0.6	0.2	1.3
Abdominal	0.7	0.9	0.5	0.1	0.4	0.6	0.5
Psychiatric	0.2	0.4	1.2	0.6	0.2	0.4	0.4
Post-traumatic head syndrome	0.0	0.1	0.1	0.1	0.1	0.1	0.1
Other	1.5	1.7	3.9	2.1	1.1	1.2	1.6
Multiple	22.1	28.0	27.0	25.6	28.1	33.2	27.9

In Figure 3.2, we compare the earnings of injured firefighters to their matched uninjured workers before and after the injury. The horizontal axis reports the quarter from injury, with zero representing the quarter of injury. The vertical axis reports the quarterly earnings. The blue line represents the earnings of uninjured controls, while the red line indicates the earnings of the injured workers. The 95-percent confidence interval of the quarterly earnings for both the injured and uninjured workers is provided.

First, we note that, despite the lack of information on the occupation of the controls, the quality of the match appears strong. The match is based on the first four quarters prior to injury, so the four quarters before injury give us the ability to test the overall match quality. While there is some separation, with the injured firefighters having slightly higher earnings, the overall difference is fairly minor. Thus, any bias that occurs from a lack of information on

Figure 3.2
Earnings of Injured Firefighters and Their Uninjured Controls Before and After Injury

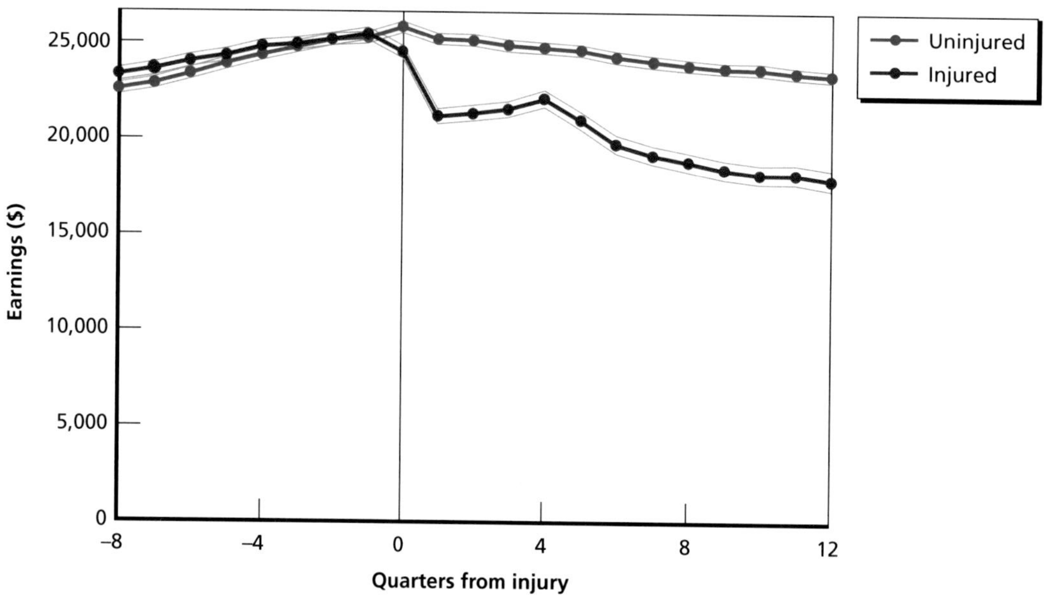

RAND *MG1018-3.2*

the occupation of the controls is likely small.[3] The 95-percent confidence intervals appear to overlap in most quarters.

The pattern of postinjury earnings for firefighters relative to the controls is different from that of the more general populations studied by RAND in previous work. There is an initial drop in wages that actually increases over the first year, possibly due to the Labor Code §4850 benefits and salary continuance they receive (see Figure 3.3). After the first year, however, the earnings drop noticeably and stay below those of the uninjured control workers. This suggests that the outcomes for firefighters are better for the first year after injury but are mostly similar to the general population in later years. The 95-percent confidence intervals are tight, and the postinjury differences are clearly statistically significant.[4]

In Figure 3.4, we report the relative employment ratios before and after injury by occupation. The horizontal axis in each panel represents quarter from injury, while the vertical axis represents the relative employment ratio of the injured workers compared to the controls. So, a relative employment ratio of, say, 0.8 in a quarter indicates that an injured worker is 20 percent less likely than uninjured controls to have positive earnings in that quarter. Each panel reports the relative employment ratios over time for a different occupation. The fact that the

[3] Note that earnings peak in the quarter of injury for both injured and control workers. We might expect earnings to increase over time for the control sample, or at least stay flat. The slight decline we observe is due to the fact that we restrict the sample to only people who are employed in the quarter of injury. There is some attrition from the labor market (or at least from our sample) over time even for the control workers, so we tend to see a declining wage profile for the controls over time.

[4] The earnings and employment for injured and uninjured workers are precisely estimated in all specifications, which is intuitive because the estimates are essentially sample means. To aid in the clarity of our figures and tables, we do not generally report significance levels in the analyses that follow, although, in virtually all cases, the postinjury earnings and employment experiences of injured workers and their matched controls are statistically different from each other.

Figure 3.3
Relative Employment Ratios Before and After Injury, by Occupation

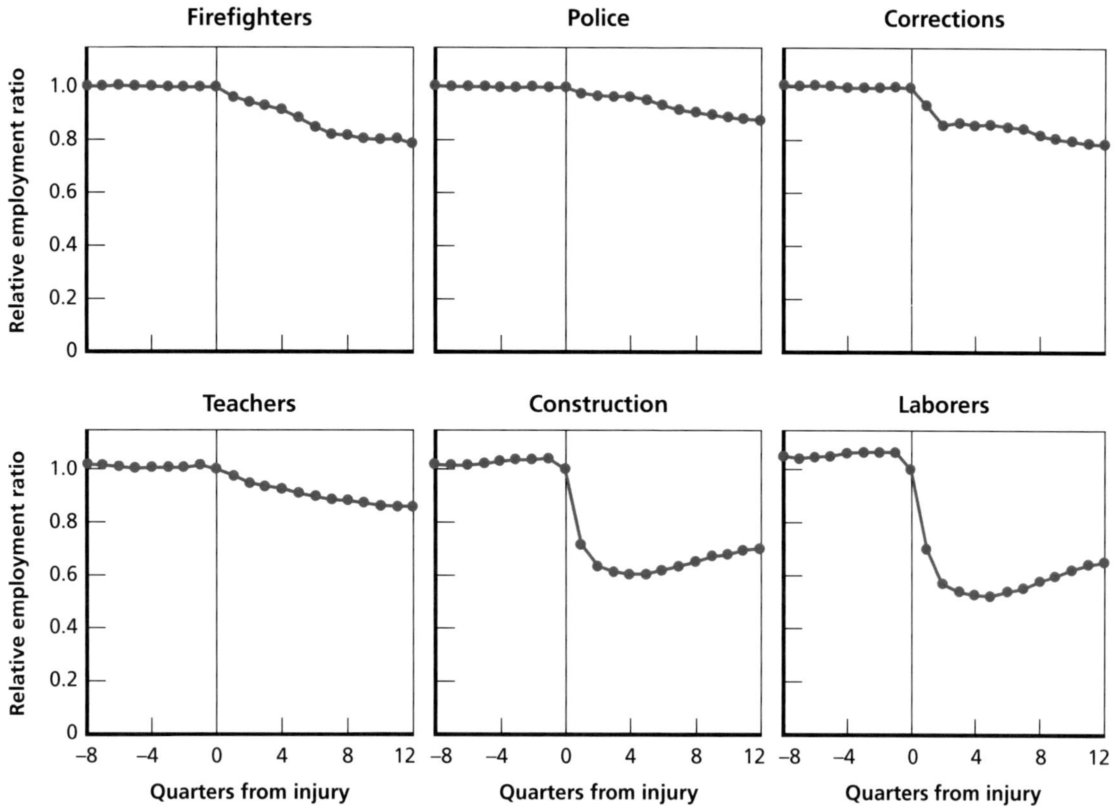

RAND *MG1018-3.3*

relative employment ratios are close to 1 for all quarters prior to injury confirms the quality of the matches across occupations.

The figure shows that the impact of an injury on employment is comparatively minor for firefighters over the first few quarters after injury. This is true for firefighters, police officers, and teachers. As discussed earlier, this is not surprising, given that these workers all have special provisions granting them additional benefits in the event of a workplace injury, benefits that are likely to be coded as earnings in our data.

The Labor Code §4850 benefits will be exhausted after a year, and, when we look past this point, the employment outcomes of firefighters decline more noticeably. In the fifth quarter after an injury, the relative employment of firefighters is 0.88—i.e., they are 12 percent less likely to be working than their uninjured controls. In the eighth quarter after an injury, this drops to about 0.82, and, by 12 quarters after, it drops to 0.79. The impact of a disabling injury on the employment of firefighters is worse than that for police officers and teachers (relative employment ratios of 0.88 and 0.86, respectively, in quarter 12) but roughly equivalent to that of corrections officers (0.79 in quarter 12).

It is clear from the figure, however, that the impact of a permanently disabling injury is considerably worse for workers in the two private-sector occupations we consider than for the public-sector workers. We see a significant and immediate drop in the relative employment of both construction workers and laborers (relative employment ratios of 0.64 and 0.57, respectively, in quarter 2). There is some recovery after the first six quarters after injury, but the long-

Figure 3.4
Proportional Wage Losses, by Occupation

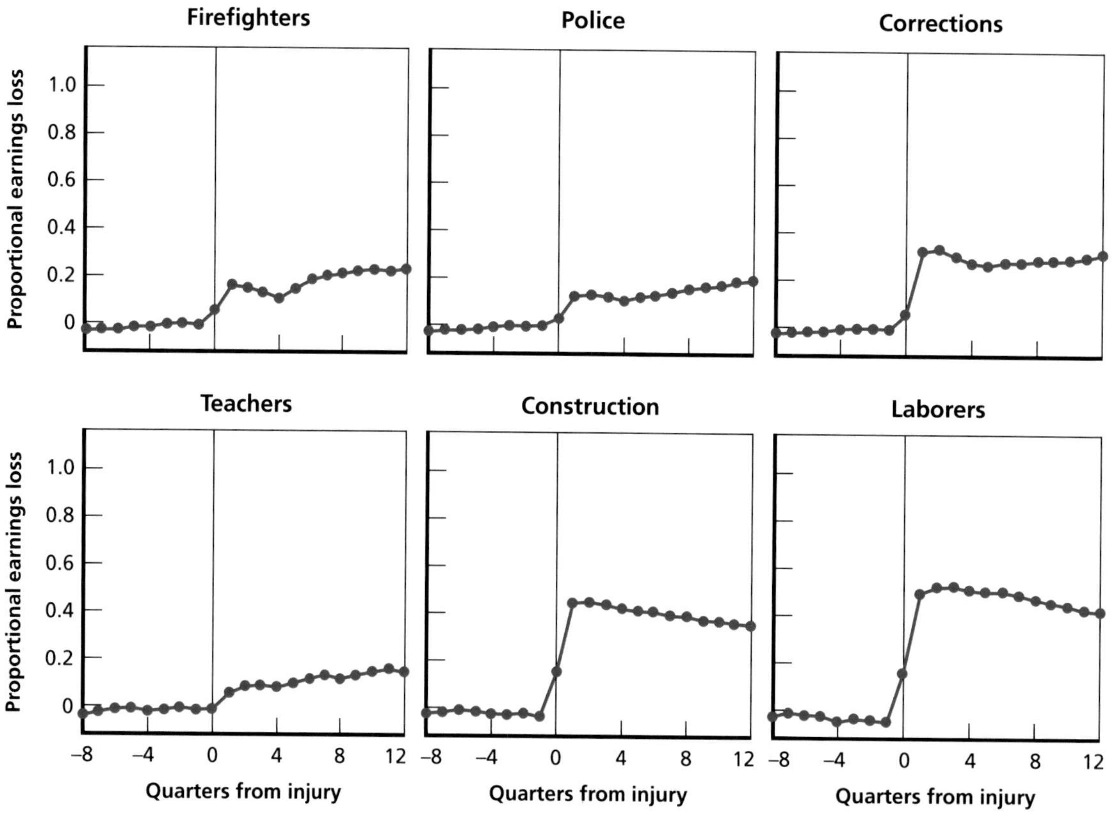

RAND *MG1018-3.4*

term effects are extreme. The relative employment ratio for construction workers in quarter 12 is 0.70, and, for laborers, it is 0.65.

As we would expect, these differences in relative employment are consistent with the differences we see in earnings losses associated with disability. Figure 3.5 reports the proportional earnings losses of workers by occupation. The figure is structured similarly to Figure 3.4, except the vertical axis in each panel represents the difference in earnings between uninjured and injured workers relative to the earnings of the uninjured workers—the proportional earnings loss. Again, the fact that proportional losses are approximately zero prior to an injury indicates the quality of the match.

Proportional losses vary by occupation. Firefighters experience proportional losses of approximately 0.23 in quarter 12. This is more than the losses of police officers (0.19) and teachers (0.14) but less than the losses of correctional officers (0.31). The long-term losses of construction workers and laborers are noticeably higher; construction workers have proportional losses of 0.35 in quarter 12, while laborers have proportional losses of 0.42.[5]

---

[5] As discussed previously, the postinjury average earnings and employment of injured and control workers are statistically different from each other. Though not reported here, we have also verified that the earnings loss and relative employment of workers are statistically different from each other. For example, the *F*-statistic for the joint hypothesis test that the average earnings losses in quarter 8 are equal across the occupations we consider is 128 ($p < 0.001$), allowing us to reject equality for all conventional significance levels.

Figure 3.5
Relative Employment Ratios of Injured Firefighters, by Injury Type

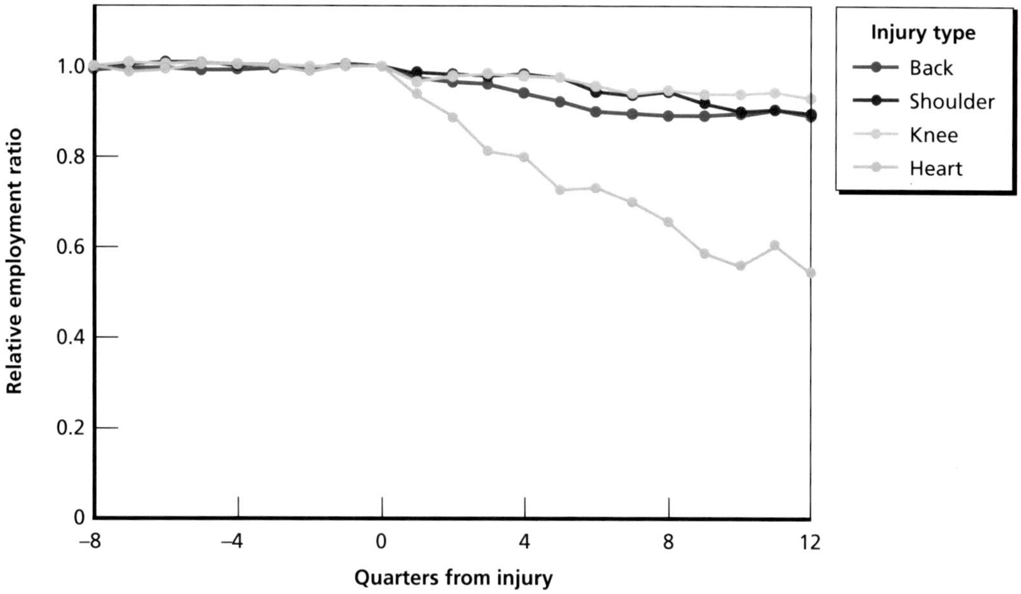

RAND *MG1018-3.5*

These figures compare the losses across occupations for all types of injuries, but we are particularly interested in the economic impact of MSDs on firefighters. Figure 3.5 reports the relative employment ratios of firefighters with four different categories of injuries: back injuries, knee injuries, shoulder injuries, and heart disease.

The figure suggests that the long-term impact of MSDs on employment for firefighters is relatively minor. The relative employment ratios of back injuries, knee injuries, and shoulder injuries are fairly similar, with knee injuries having slightly less impact. In quarter 12, the relative employment ratio of firefighters with back injuries is 0.89; with shoulder injuries, it is 0.90; and, with knee injuries, it is 0.93. Not surprisingly, these employment differences translate into similar differences in earnings losses. If we compute the proportional losses for firefighters with these injury types, we find that the proportional losses in quarter 12 are 0.11 for firefighters with back injuries, 0.11 for firefighters with shoulder injuries, and just 0.04 for firefighters with knee injuries.

The impact of these injuries on earnings and employment for firefighters is still significant, but it is relatively minor compared to the losses experienced by other occupations. Moreover, they pale in comparison to the losses experienced by firefighters with heart disease. The figure shows that the relative employment ratio for firefighters with heart disease falls to less than 0.6 in the third year after the date of injury (in the case of a chronic condition, such as heart disease, this is probably better referred to as the date of disability onset). The relative employment ratio in quarter 12 for firefighters with heart disease is 0.55, and the proportional earnings losses are 0.60.[6]

These results suggest that, while the average earnings losses for firefighters who experience permanent disabilities is substantial—with approximately 20-percent earnings loss three years

[6] Because heart disease is presumed job related, there is controversy about the extent to which the cases we observe are truly occupational, and we have no way to determine this in our data.

after the date of injury—this loss level masks considerable heterogeneity in outcomes across different injury types. In particular, the earnings losses associated with back injuries and other common types of injuries appear to be relatively minor. As a point of comparison, the average proportional loss in quarter 12 for construction workers with back injuries is 0.38, and, for laborers, it is 0.46.

Our earlier analysis of BLS data indicated that the differences in frequency and severity of injuries between firefighters and other workers were considerably more pronounced at older ages. Figure 3.6 reports the relative employment ratios two years after injury (i.e., in quarter 8) by age and occupation. The relative employment ratios are reported on the horizontal axis. Each set of bars indicates the relative employment ratios for the different age categories by occupation.

From the figure, it is clear that the impact of disability on employment of firefighters is less severe for younger workers. Firefighters in the 25–34 and 35–44 age categories experience negligible losses in employment. In the 45–54 age category, however, the relative employment ratio drops to 0.83. For the oldest employment category, the 55–60 group, the relative employment ratio two years after injury is 0.42.[7]

Data for the other occupations suggest that the impact of disability is worse for the oldest workers, but the relationship is not as strong. The impact on police officers is quite similar to that on firefighters for all age categories except the 55–60 category, in which the impact on

Figure 3.6
Relative Employment Ratios Two Years After Injury, by Age and Occupation, for All Injuries

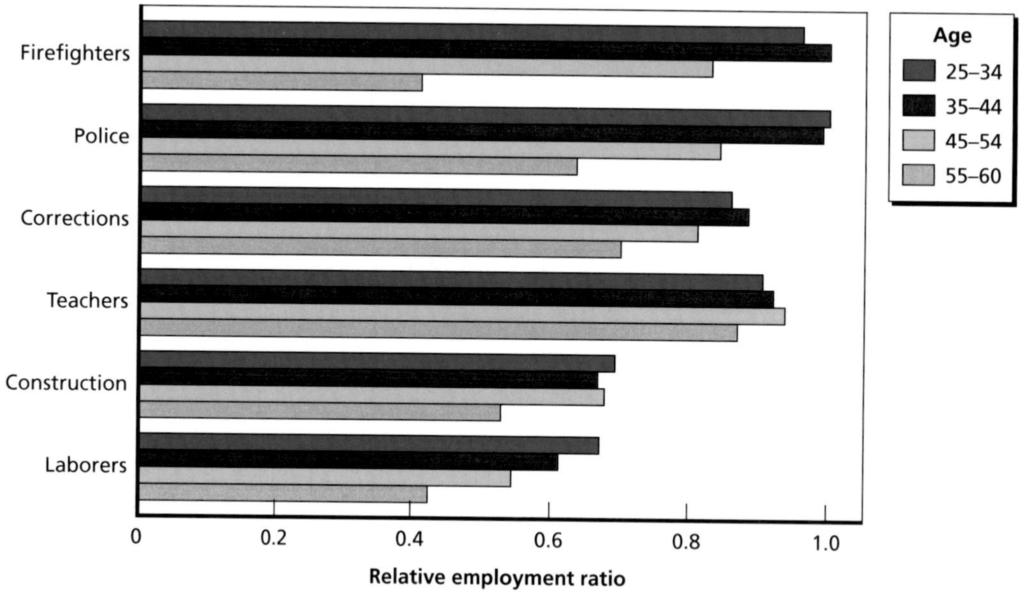

RAND *MG1018-3.6*

[7] An important limitation to this analysis is that, as with occupation, we do not observe the age of uninjured workers. Conditioning on the age of the injured workers without conditioning on the age of the uninjured controls raises the possibility of bias. This occurs because our match procedure likely matches older injured workers to younger uninjured workers and vice versa. To test whether this might have biased our findings in any significant way, we compared the probability of employment two years after injury (that is, the level of employment without conditioning on the employment of the controls) across age categories and occupations. We found the same general results, suggesting to us that any bias is not driving our results.

firefighters is considerably more pronounced. Teachers exhibit very little relationship between age and the impact of disability, perhaps because the nature of the work is among the least physically demanding of the occupations considered here. For construction workers and laborers, the relative employment ratios decline steadily with age, but they start from a much lower baseline, so the difference is smaller. The relative employment ratios for the oldest firefighters are as low as those for the oldest laborers and construction workers, indicating just how pronounced the effect is.

As we saw before, the impact of a disability on the employment outcomes of firefighters varies considerably across different types of injuries. In Figure 3.7, we compare the relative employment ratios of workers with a back injury by age and occupation.

The figure shows that the differences in employment outcomes across age and occupation for back injuries are similar to those for all injuries. The general pattern is similar for firefighters. The two younger age categories exhibit little adverse impact of disability on employment. Workers in the 45–54 age category have a relative employment ratio of 0.88, but it drops to 0.51 for the firefighters 55–60. This difference is more pronounced than for any other occupation except the oldest laborers, whose relative employment ratio drops to 0.24.

In our previous discussion, we noted that one factor distinguishing public-safety employment from other occupations is the availability of disability retirement (which is available at earlier ages and has favorable tax status compared to regular retirement). Safety employees, including firefighters, also have more options in terms of early retirement. Thus, some of the decline in employment for the older workers could be due to an increased propensity to retire. It is noteworthy, however, that police officers have similar options in terms of disability retirement, but we do not see the same impact of disability on relative employment for the oldest police officers. This is at least suggestive that the physical nature of firefighting has a particularly adverse impact on the oldest firefighters. This is consistent with the findings of

Figure 3.7
Relative Employment Ratios for Workers with Back Injuries Two Years After Injury, by Age and Occupation

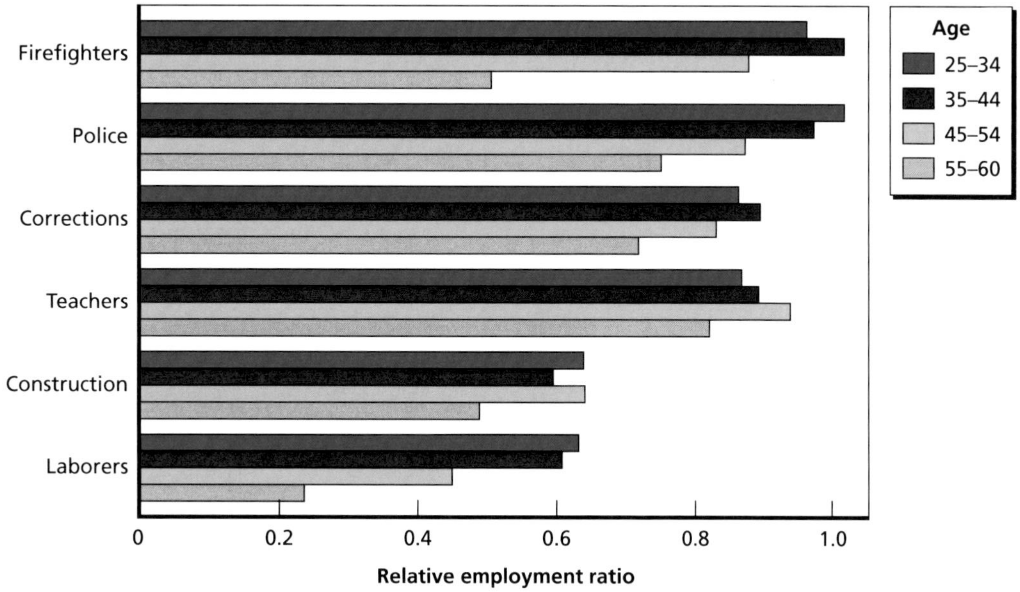

RAND *MG1018-3.7*

LaTourrette, Loughran, and Seabury (2008), which suggest that older firefighters are more susceptible to permanent disability after an injury.

Summary

Our earlier analysis of BLS data suggested that the frequency and severity of MSDs is higher for firefighters than other workers. In this chapter, we studied the impact of permanently disabling injuries on the long-term earnings and employment of firefighters. Our results suggest that firefighters do experience significant long-term earnings losses and employment losses several years after a disability. Nevertheless, the impact of MSDs—back injuries in particular—seems much more moderate for firefighters than for other employees. Firefighters age 55 and older appear to represent an exception to this finding, however. The oldest firefighters in our sample experience employment losses as bad, on average, as those of workers in any of the private-sector occupations we studied. Nevertheless, considering the enhanced compensation available to firefighters, it seems likely that the economic impact of a disabling injury for firefighters is less, on average, than for most other workers.

CHAPTER FOUR

Assessing the Impact of Reforms on Disability Ratings for Firefighters

In this chapter, we study the impact of recent reforms to the permanent-disability rating system in California on firefighters with MSDs.

Background

Here, we discuss the change to the disability rating system introduced by California Senate Bill (SB) 899. While the reforms were broad in terms of scope and made many changes, we highlight two in particular. In particular, we focus on how the introduction of a new basis for disability ratings led to a decline in the average ratings and an increase in the number of injuries that received no positive rating at all, and how new apportionment rules led to a decline in ratings in which there were questions about the causality of the disability. Our discussion is limited in scope, with the primary purpose being to highlight how the reforms might have differentially affected workers with MSDs. For more thorough discussions of the reforms and the changes made to the rating system, see, for example, CHSWC (2006, 2007).

We begin with some background on the system for evaluating disability severity in California for permanent disabilities. California is somewhat unique in that every PPD claim in workers' compensation is assigned a disability rating, a number from 1 to 100 that is designed to reflect the severity of an injured worker's disability. A rating of 0 indicates no disability, while a rating of 100 means the worker is unable to work. The disability rating is based on one or more physicians' medical reports describing the nature of the injury and is assigned only after the worker has recovered to the extent possible and the injury is declared "permanent and stationary."

The disability rating is adjusted to reflect a number of factors, including age and occupation, but is primarily based on the type of injury and a physician's evaluation of severity. These ratings directly translate into the amount of benefits that a worker receives. A worker receives a weekly PPD benefit that is based on his or her weekly wage, but the number of weeks for which the worker receives these benefits is a convex function of the disability rating.

SB 899, signed into law on April 19, 2004, made sweeping changes to the state workers' compensation system. These changes included a massive overhaul to the system for evaluating the severity of permanent disabilities. Motivated in part by evidence of persistent inconsistencies, inequities, and subjectivity that marred the old rating system (see Reville, Seabury, et al., 2005), as well as consistent complaints that it promoted litigation, SB 899 adopted the American Medical Association's *Guides to the Evaluation of Permanent Impairment* (AMA Guides) (Labor Code §4660[b][1]). The AMA Guides are widely considered to be a more objective rating system and are used in multiple state workers' compensation systems. In addition to the AMA Guides, the new reforms required physicians to make a determination of the apportionment of disability to work-related factors for every permanent-disability claim (revised Labor Code §4463[a]).

Both the adoption of the AMA Guides and the new apportionment rules led to a substantial reduction in the size of permanent-disability ratings, thereby reducing the size of permanent-disability awards. The adoption of the AMA Guides led to a reduction because the average rating in the AMA Guides is lower than the rating assigned to a similar rating evaluated using the Permanent Disability Rating Schedule (PDRS). Neuhauser (2007) found that the average permanent-disability rating in California after AMA Guide adoption was 41.7 percent lower than under the PDRS prior to adoption.

In addition to the resulting direct reduction to ratings, the AMA guidelines are more likely to yield zero ratings for certain injuries. The California PDRS was often labeled a more "subjective" rating system, in large part because it allowed ratings to be based solely on a physician's assessment of work restrictions. This meant that very few permanent injuries were given a zero rating under the old system. This is particularly true of nonspecific muscle or joint pain that has no identifiable organic cause of disability but for which a physician might recommend limiting certain physical activities as part of treatment. The AMA Guides, however, do not prescribe a rating based solely on a physician's assessment of work limitations. Thus, any injury that would have been rated solely on the basis of work restrictions would receive a zero rating under the new system. Given that MSDs are less likely to have objective signs of disability, we expect them to have a greater fraction of zero ratings.

The introduction of the new apportionment rules also led to a decline in disability ratings. SB 899 repealed the previous rules on apportionment (Labor Code §§4663 and 4750) and added the new requirement that "apportionment of permanent disability shall be based on causation" (revised Labor Code §4663[a]). Specifically, the rule requires that physicians determine the percentage of causation that can be directly attributed to job-related factors, and the disability rating is reduced by the fraction that is not.[1] For more detail, see CHSWC (2007). These new rules have had a significant impact on permanent-disability cases. In particular, 9.8 percent of all permanent-disability cases included apportionment in 2006, leading to an average reduction in ratings of 40.1 percent (CHSWC, 2007). Overall, the apportioning of permanent disability to causation reduced total PPD benefit payments by almost 6 percent (CHSWC, 2007).

This rule could have uncertain ramifications for workers who suffer permanently disabling MSDs. In any injury, there is difficulty in establishing causation for disease and complex injury cases, and there is an absence of precision in apportioning the contribution of various causes (Guidotti, 2006). The process is even more complex for MSDs, because they often involve many factors and might lack organic evidence of disability (Guidotti, 2002). This

---

[1] More precisely, Labor Code §4663(c) states, in part, that

> [a] physician shall make an apportionment determination by finding what approximate percentage of the permanent disability was caused by the direct result of injury arising out of and occurring in the course of employment and what approximate percentage of the permanent disability was caused by other factors both before and subsequent to the industrial injury, including prior industrial injuries. . . .

Furthermore, Labor Code §4664(a) states that "[t]he employer shall only be liable for the percentage of permanent disability directly caused by the injury arising out of and occurring in the course of employment."

uncertainty could lead to inequities in the apportionment process, resulting in what is essentially the same injury with the same risk factors receiving different apportionment. If MSDs are both more common and more disabling for firefighters, the apportionment rules could have a greater impact on them. Thus, the way apportionment is applied to firefighter MSDs could have a significant impact on the adequacy of the compensation they receive.

Analysis of Disability Rating Trends

Our analysis in this chapter uses the same DEU data described in our analysis of the earnings and employment outcomes of firefighters. We include the same set of firefighters, as well as the five other occupations considered previously. We compare trends in the average disability rating for workers injured in different years.[2]

In our analysis in this section, we focus on the actual rating from the DEU. The DEU rates many different types of medical reports, but we restrict this analysis to reports from randomly selected qualified medical evaluator (QME) panels. We make this restriction because the other reports, particularly consult reports made on behalf of applicant- or defense-selected physicians, have been shown to exhibit biases in the ratings (Reville, Seabury, et al., 2005; Seabury, Reville, and Neuhauser, 2006). This fact, combined with the fact that SB 899 placed limits on the ability of different parties to select physicians for the purposes of ratings, we feel that the QME reports will provide us with the most accurate picture of rating trends over time.

Figure 4.1 illustrates the average permanent-disability rating by occupation from 2000 through 2007. The vertical axis reports the average disability rating, and the horizontal axis reports the injury year. The average rating reported in the figure is calculated across all injury types. Two different trends are reported in each panel. The first excludes all cases with a zero rating, while the second includes them and treats them as zero. This distinction helps separate the impact of the adoption of the AMA Guides into two effects: a change in the average rating for rated claims and an increase in the number of claims receiving a nonzero rating.

The figure confirms that there was a steep decline in the average disability rating for firefighters. The average ratings for firefighters consistently exceeded 20 prior to 2004 but fell to closer to ten by 2007. When zero ratings are included, the decline is even sharper, with average ratings below ten by 2007.

There are two other interesting findings from Figure 4.1. The first is that, while firefighters experienced a pronounced drop in average ratings, the decline was actually less pronounced than for the other occupations. This appears to be due at least in part to the fact that the average rating for firefighters is lower than that for the other occupations in the sample. The average rating for firefighters at the end of the series appears closer to that for the other occupations. The second finding is that the impact of the zero ratings appears to be larger for firefighters, and for public-safety occupations in general, than for the other occupations. That is, the difference between the lines with and without the zero ratings is greater for firefighters than for the other occupations.

[2] The amount of time from date of injury until the date when an injury is declared permanent and stationary and becomes eligible for a permanent-disability rating varies considerably but can be a matter of years. Thus, even though the new rating schedule took effect on January 1, 2005, some workers with injuries prior to that date will still be affected.

Figure 4.1
Trends in Permanent-Disability Ratings, by Occupation

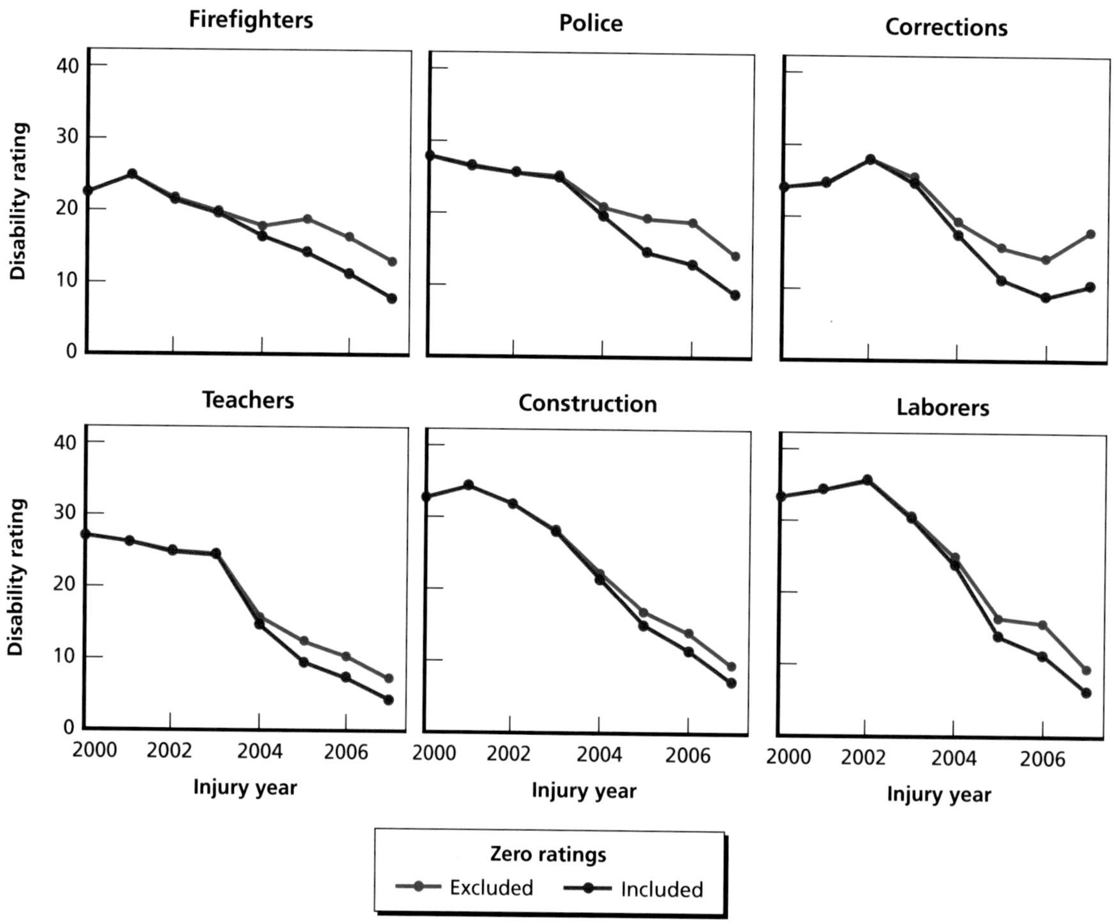

RAND *MG1018-4.1*

In Figure 4.2, we report the average permanent-disability rating by occupation from 2000 through 2007 but restrict the analysis to back injuries only. As before, the vertical axis reports the average disability rating, and the horizontal axis reports the injury year. In this case, we report the trend only for cases with a positive rating. The reason for this is that the DEU does not assign a disability type to the zero-rated claims; thus, we cannot compare the zero-rated claims for specific disabilities.

The figure generally confirms the findings from Figure 4.1. Firefighters with back injuries experienced a clear decline in their average permanent-disability ratings later in the time period covered by the sample. The average rating for other occupations was higher than for firefighters prior to the reforms, however, and they experienced a steeper decline in the average rating. By 2007, the average rating for firefighters with back injuries was generally comparable to the average rating for other occupations.

The fact that the impact of the inclusion of zero-rated claims has a bigger impact on firefighters than on those in other occupations suggests that firefighters have a higher fraction of claims with a zero rating. To verify this, we restricted our sample to those that were rated under the new disability rating schedule and compared the fraction of those cases with a zero rating by occupation. These findings are reported in Table 4.1.

Figure 4.2
Trends in Permanent-Disability Ratings, by Occupation, Back Injuries Only

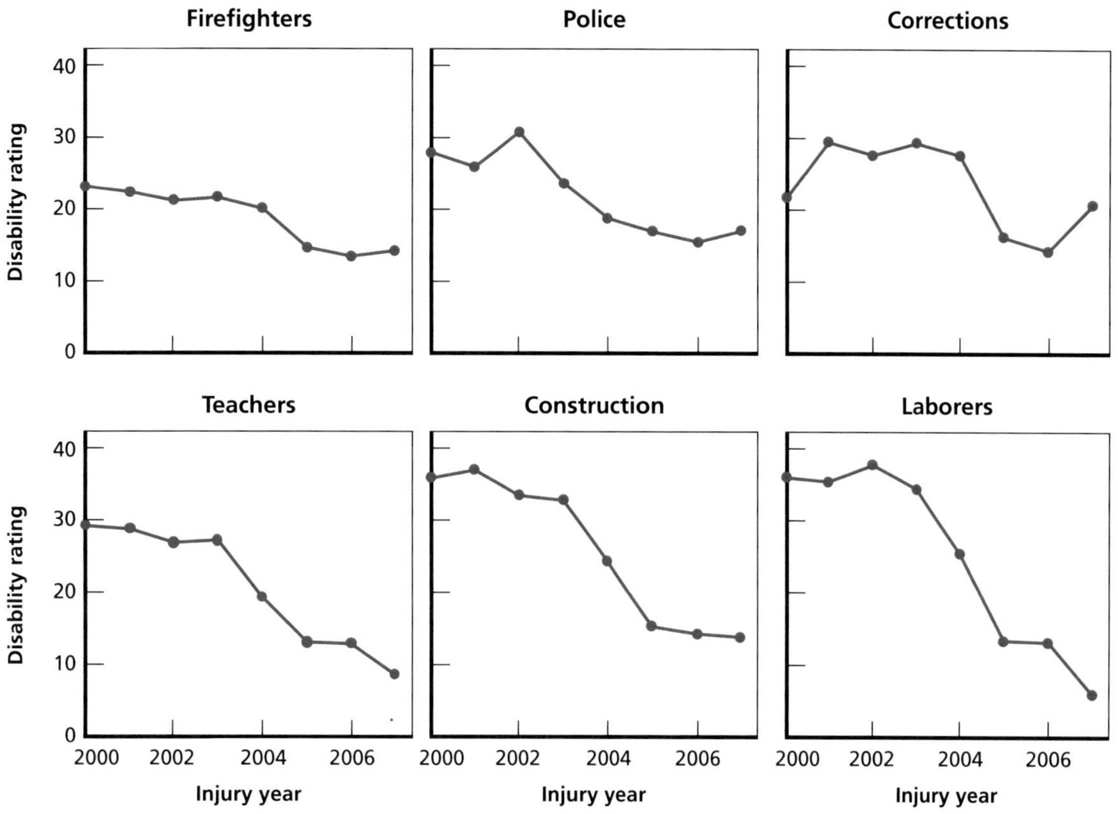

RAND *MG1018-4.2*

Table 4.1
Share of Zero-Rated Claims, by Occupation

Occupation	Fraction with a Zero Rating	Relative Employment Ratio: Rated Claim	Relative Employment Ratio: Zero-Rated Claim	Proportional Wage Loss: Rated Claim	Proportional Wage Loss: Zero-Rated Claim	No. of Observations
Firefighters	0.24	0.81	0.93	0.19	0.05	1,289
Police	0.21	0.91	0.96	0.14	0.03	2,637
Corrections	0.22	0.85	0.98	0.30	0.08	981
Teachers	0.19	0.87	0.93	0.14	−0.01	1,780
Construction	0.10	0.68	0.92	0.36	0.13	2,908
Laborers	0.10	0.61	0.74	0.46	0.35	1,721

NOTE: The table reports the share of zero-rated claims and average economic outcomes for rated and zero-rated claims by occupation. The data include only those workers injured and evaluated under the new (i.e., post–SB 899) disability rating schedule. The economic outcomes are evaluated in the second year after injury (quarter 8).

The left column of the table reports the fraction of claims with a zero rating in each occupation. We see that firefighters indeed have a larger share of zero-rated claims, 0.24, nearly one-quarter. The share for all public workers is high, with shares of 0.21 for police officers,

0.22 for corrections, and 0.19 for teachers. This is compared to 0.10 for the two private-sector occupations we consider.

The next two columns of the table report the relative employment ratio for workers with a rated claim or a zero-rated claim, respectively. Workers with a zero-rated claim consistently have higher relative employment ratios than workers with a rated claim. In fact, the relative employment ratio is greater than 90 percent for all occupations except for laborers. The next two columns report the proportional earnings losses for workers with a rated claim or a zero-rated claim, respectively. As with the case of the relative employment ratios, these figures indicate that the zero-rated claims have comparably minor reduction in earnings on average, generally less than 10 percent. In fact, the only category in which workers with the zero-rated claims appear to experience significant adverse employment outcomes is the laborers.[3]

Apportionment and Disability Ratings

We use the DEU data to examine the impact of apportionment on the disability ratings of firefighters. The DEU data contain information on apportionment in nonrepresented cases, and apportionment is relevant only for workers rated under the post–SB 899 schedule. Thus, we restrict our sample to workers rated under the new schedule in unrepresented cases.[4]

We are interested in two dimensions of apportionment: the *frequency* with which it is applied and the *severity* of the impact on disability ratings for injured workers. Frequency is measured simply as the fraction of cases that involve some apportionment. The severity is measured as the percentage reduction in the disability rating that results from the apportionment finding. We evaluate severity for cases with apportionment and overall.

Table 4.2 compares the frequency and severity of apportionment in claims involving back injuries and all other injuries by occupation. The fraction of cases with an apportionment finding in claims with back injuries is consistently higher than the fraction of cases with apportionment in other injury claims. About 15 percent of firefighter back-injury claims involved apportionment, compared to 8 percent of all other claims. This disparity is even higher for the non–public-safety workers, with 16 percent of back-injury claims made by laborers involving apportionment, compared to just 4 percent of all other claims.

The severity of apportionment conditional on an apportionment finding is higher for back-injury claims than other claims for firefighters. Firefighters with apportionment in a back-injury claim see their rating reduced by 36 percent on average, compared to 25 percent for other injuries. This finding is not consistent, however, when we look across the different occupations. In most other occupations, the severity of apportionment is higher in the other claims than in the back-injury claims.[5] It is unclear why there is no clear pattern, except perhaps that

[3] It is unclear whether this is an anomaly or an indication that the zero-rated claims are applied to more severe injuries for lower-skilled workers. While beyond the scope of this study, we feel that this issue merits further research.

[4] Because apportionment is something that could be litigated, it seems likely that the frequency of apportionment is greater in cases with attorney representation than without. It is unclear whether the differences across occupation and injury types that we consider in this section would be affected by this selection. Ultimately, this is something that can be answered only in future work.

[5] These differences are statistically significant. That is, if we conduct an F-test of the difference in severity across occupations in back cases or in other cases, we reject the null hypothesis that the differences are jointly zero ($p < 0.01$).

Table 4.2
Frequency and Severity of Apportionment, by Occupation and Injury

	Fraction with Apportionment		Average Reduction in Apportioned Cases (%)		Average Reduction in All Cases (%)	
Occupation	Back Injuries	Other Injuries	Back Injuries	Other Injuries	Back Injuries	Other Injuries
Firefighters	0.15	0.08	36	25	6	2
Police	0.17	0.10	27	34	5	4
Corrections	0.17	0.12	40	39	7	5
Teachers	0.18	0.09	33	41	6	4
Construction	0.14	0.04	30	34	4	2
Laborers	0.16	0.04	29	41	5	2

the nature of work differs sufficiently across the different occupations to prevent any general relationship to be found.

When we examine the severity in the average case, we see that the average reduction is consistently higher in back-injury claims than in other injury claims. The average reduction in ratings is fairly small, with less than a 10 percent reduction in every occupation type for back injuries or other injuries. This masks the considerable reductions in cases in which apportionment is applied, however, and these are cases that disproportionately involve MSDs.

Summary

In this section, we studied how recent reforms to the permanent-disability rating system in California affected firefighters, particularly those with MSDs. We found that firefighters experienced significant declines in average ratings as a result of the new schedule being adopted. The biggest impact on firefighters, however, appears to have been a disproportionately large fraction of cases that receive no disability rating. It is unclear exactly why that is, though we speculate that one possible explanation is that firefighters were more likely to be disabled under the work-restriction guidelines of the old California schedule than under the new system using the AMA Guides. It is possible that more firefighters file claims that cannot be rated under the AMA Guides because these guidelines do not contain these kinds of subjective restrictions. Apportionment has led to a small reduction in the average rating for firefighters, as it has for other workers. But, while the effects are small on average, there is typically a large reduction in ratings whenever apportionment is applied.

CHAPTER FIVE

Evaluating the Impact of Medical Reforms on Employment Outcomes for Firefighters

In this chapter, we evaluate the impact of medical reforms on employment outcomes for firefighters by employing a number of indirect methods. First, we perform a systematic review of the literature and analyze MEPS to assess the utilization rates of chiropractic and physical therapy. We also review the existing evidence on the effectiveness of long-term use of these therapies. Second, we employ data from the DEU and EDD to evaluate firefighter employment before and after the implementation of the reforms.

Background

As part of a number of workers' compensation reforms in California that were first introduced in California SB 228 and later in SB 899, several labor-code sections were adopted that affect medical treatment after a workplace injury. In response to skyrocketing doctor of chiropractic (DC) and physical therapist (PT) costs, which comprised roughly 37 percent of all California workers' compensation outpatient payments prior to the reforms (Swedlow, 2005), Labor Code §4604.5 was adopted. This new section imposes a limit of 24 visits to a DC or PT for the life of a workers' compensation claim occurring on or after January 1, 2004, unless the employer authorizes additional treatments. This provision is of particular relevance for workers with an MSD because chiropractic care and physical therapy are common treatments for MSD ailments.

Another relevant aspect of the reforms was the shift in decisionmaking for medical treatment beyond the 24-visit cap from the medical care provider to the employer. This shift is enforced by Labor Code §4062.9, which repeals the presumption of correctness of the treating physician. Labor Code §4610 requires employers to adopt utilization review systems consistent with the American College of Occupational and Environmental (ACOEM) guidelines or some other approved set of guidelines.

For a soft-tissue low back injury, one of the most common work-related MSDs, ACOEM guidelines recommend two or less PT visits and 12 DC visits, both of which are well below the new limit. With the ability of employers to authorize additional treatment above the cap when deemed necessary by utilization review, the effect on injured workers is not clear. However, since the enactment of these provisions, DC and PT utilization rates and costs have reduced dramatically (Swedlow, 2005).

Despite the large cost and utilization-rate reductions, the overall social-welfare effects of the cap are unclear, particularly for firefighters. Given the high proportion of MSDs experienced by firefighters relative to other occupations, a cap on DC and PT treatments might be disproportionately felt by this sector of the workforce. First, as we mentioned earlier, MSDs often lack organic evidence of disability (Guidotti, 2002). This might prevent some firefighters from receiving beneficial treatment above and beyond the 24-visit limit because of a lack of evidence to justify additional treatment. Second, because MSDs are often a cumulative injury, it is more challenging to provide evidence documenting the injury within the standard timeline for discovery. Furthermore, due to the physical nature of the job and the higher MSD risks and severity, firefighters might simply have a higher demand for DC and PT treatments than workers in other occupations, rendering them more affected by these new provisions.

To evaluate the impact of the reforms, we first focus on determining average utilization rates for DC and PT treatments. To accomplish this task, we search the literature and analyze MEPS. Determining average utilization rates of DC and PT treatments will allow us to identify how many injured workers we would expect to be affected if utilization in California workers' compensation cases were comparable to that of the general population.

Next, we perform a systematic literature review to assess the existing evidence on the effectiveness of DC and PT treatments, with a focus on long-term treatments, compared to alternative methods. This analysis helps inform us as to what we expect the impact of the reforms to be if a significant portion of firefighters are not able to receive treatments. Finally, we utilize DEU and EDD data to analyze the employment outcomes of firefighters before and after the implementation of the reforms. If the reforms have had a significant adverse effect on the ability of firefighters to obtain necessary DC and PT treatments, we would expect to see worsening employment outcomes for this group.

Study of Existing Work on the Use and Effectiveness of Chiropractic Care and Physical Therapy

Methods

We performed a systematic review of the literature to evaluate the existing evidence on the average utilization and effectiveness of DC and PT treatments. We focused our search on eight high-quality journals within MEDLINE using search terms chosen to identify relevant papers by addressing type of care, type of injury, and outcome measures. Table 5.1 reports the specific journals and terms we used and the total number of papers searched. Other papers found through secondary searches or by reviewing separate papers were included in our summary as necessary. In total, our search identified 5,797 possible papers.

In addition to the literature review, we use MEPS to estimate the average utilization rates among individuals who went to a DC or PT. MEPS is a nationally representative survey conducted by the Agency for Healthcare Research and Quality (AHRQ) designed to measure health care insurance, utilization, and expenditures. While MEPS is a nationally representative sample and not specific to California, it allows us to estimate average utilization rates for individuals with an MSD injury and for individuals injured at work. With the survey data, we can identify the proportion of individuals who went to a DC or PT more than 24 times for an MSD, helping us understand how binding the cap is, assuming average levels of utilization.

To evaluate the effectiveness of DC and PT treatments, we review the literature for evidence on three classes of outcomes: (1) health outcomes (e.g., disability or impairment), (2) RTW, and (3) cost-effectiveness. Assessing the health effects of DC and PT treatment is important in order to identify whether treatments improve health outcomes for workers with

Table 5.1
Systematic Literature Review Search Terms and Journal List

Search Term		JAMA	NEJM	AJPH	AIM	JOEM	JOR	AJIM	Spine	Total
Treatment	Chiropractic	34	42	18	19	2	2	1	114	232
	Physical therapy	491	312	65	278	20	34	18	741	1,959
	Occupational therapy	72	37	16	19	97	57	64	99	461
	Spinal manipulation	10	13	5	26	0	1	0	144	199
Injury	Musculoskeletal disorder	12	0	8	7	50	67	97	56	297
	Chronic pain	138	128	9	117	34	53	20	803	1,302
	Soft-tissue injury	10	2	0	2	5	0	6	56	81
	Low back pain	70	59	14	49	54	72	50	0	368
Outcomes and occupation	Return to work	16	5	7	9	47	109	40	187	420
	Absenteeism	36	14	47	26	151	15	38	64	391
	Firefighters	0	8	6	1	39	1	32	0	87
Total		889	620	195	553	499	411	366	2,264	5,797

NOTE: JAMA = *Journal of the American Medical Association*. NEJM = *New England Journal of Medicine*. AJPH = *American Journal of Public Health*. AIM = *Annals of Internal Medicine*. JEOM = *Journal of Occupational and Environmental Medicine*. JOR = *Journal of Occupational Rehabilitation*. AJIM = *American Journal of Industrial Medicine*.

MSDs more than treatments by alternative options, such as a general practitioner, particularly for long-term treatments. However, despite accepted definitions of *clinical significance* (see, e.g., Goldby et al., 2006, and Cherkin, Deyo, et al., 1998), interpreting changes in commonly used health outcomes, such as the Oswestry Disability Index or the Roland-Morris Disability Questionnaire, in a policy-evaluation framework is challenging. Therefore, we also evaluate papers that assess return-to-work outcomes for workers who receive DC and PT treatments because returning injured workers to work is of primary importance. Finally, we include papers that assess the cost-effectiveness of DC and PT treatments relative to other methods because cost-effectiveness is one of the most useful metrics with which to evaluate this policy from a social-welfare perspective.

Chiropractic and Physical-Therapy Utilization Analysis

Literature Review. It is unclear how many workers should be affected by the cap on chiropractic and physical therapy. For instance, 80 to 90 percent of patients with acute low back pain, one of the most prevalent work-related MSDs and the most common reason for visiting a DC or PT (Hurwitz, Morgenstern, Harber, et al., 2002; Torstensen et al., 1998), will recover and be back to work within six to eight weeks (Frank et al., 1996).[1] However, 8 to 10 percent of those with acute pain will end up with chronic low back pain (Frank et al., 1996). In these cases, long-term treatment past the 24-visit cap might be necessary. In this section, we summarize the results of our systematic literature review on utilization to develop a better understanding of average usage.

When reviewing utilization studies, we focused on the type of care provided; the sample analyzed, including injury type and geographic location; and mean and median utilization rates. Table 5.2 summarizes the final 12 papers we selected. Of the 12 papers selected, five focus on chiropractic utilization, three on chiropractic and physical therapy, and four on physical therapy. The papers include data from U.S. nationally representative samples; data from specific states, including California, as well as international samples in Canada and Taiwan; and workers' compensation utilization rates. Sample sizes range from 160 to more than 600,000.

Shekelle and Brook (1991) provided the first set of population-based estimates of chiropractor utilization using data from the RAND Health Insurance Experiment. They estimated a median and mean number of visits per year for individuals who went to a chiropractor at least one time of seven and 11.5, respectively. A significant finding of this paper is that chiropractic use has a substantial tail to the right. Specifically, it finds that 2 percent of the sample consumed 10 percent of the total number of visits. They also note that chiropractors accounted for about twice as many visits for back pain as did physicians when compared to a previous study analyzing the National Medical Ambulatory Care Survey between 1975 and 1980 (Murt et al., 1986).

In subsequent work, Shekelle, Markovich, and Louie (1995b) further utilized RAND Health Insurance Experiment data and estimated that, of the 3,105 adults in the sample, 686 had episodes of back-pain care and the mean and median numbers of visits to a chiropractor were 10.4 and five, respectively. In another study that provided nationally representative esti-

[1] The most common MSDs treated by DCs and PTs involve back injuries. Patients with chronic low back pain represent a significant proportion of back-injury treatments and dominate the total proportion of those patients seeking long-term care. Other common MSDs treated by DCs and PTs are neck pain, carpal-tunnel syndrome, and other injuries caused by sprains, strains, and tears.

Table 5.2
Chiropractic and Physical-Therapy Utilization Studies

Study	Treatment	Injury	Data	Sample Size	Utilization Estimates
Hurwitz, Coulter, et al. (1998)	DC	All injuries treated by a DC	Chiropractors sampled from 5 U.S. and 1 Canadian site	131 chiropractors and 1,916 patients	Mean no. of visits for low back pain ranged from 10.5 to 21.3, with medians ranging from 4 to 10. Mean no. of visits for all conditions ranged from 9.6 to 16.4, with an overall mean of 12.4, and medians ranged from 4 to 9.5, with an overall median of 7.
Shekelle and Brook (1991)	DC	All injuries treated by a DC	RAND Health Insurance Experiment	5,279	395 different persons used 7,873 chiropractic services for a visit rate of 41 per 100 person-years and rate of use of 7.5 percent. The median and mean numbers of visits per year were 7 and 11.5, respectively.
Eisenberg, Kessler, et al. (1993)	DC	All	Telephone interviews in a national sample of adults 18 years of age or older in 1990	1,539	10% of the sample had used DC services in the previous month, with a mean number of visits per user of 13.
Tsauo et al. (2009)	DC	Work-related MSDs	Subjects from a medical center and regional hospital in Taiwan who were 18–65 years old and had a recent MSD injury	160	53% of the sample received PT. Of those, 70.7% received short-term treatment (<30 days) and 29.3% received long-term treatment (≥30 days). The number of sessions for the treatment groups was 7.8 ± 9.0, with a median of 6. Subjects in the short-term group received 3.6 ± 2.9 sessions, and those in the long-term group received 18.0 ± 12.9 sessions.
Carey, Freburger, et al. (2009)	DC and PT	Chronic low back pain	Noninstitutionalized adults 21 years and older in North Carolina with chronic low back pain identified by a stratified probability sample of North Carolina telephone numbers	732	Of the patients who sought care (590 of 732), the mean number of visits to a DC was 20.8 (95% CI = 16.4–25.2), and the mean number of visits to a PT was 15.6 (95% CI = 11.9–19.3). 26.9% (95% CI = 22.8–31.0) of care-seekers went to a DC, and 29.7% (95% CI = 25.7–33.8) went to a PT.
Shekelle, Markovich, and Louie (1995b)	DC	Back-pain care	RAND Health Insurance Experiment	3,105; 686 with episodes of back-pain care	Mean no. of visits to a DC per episode of back pain was 10.4, with a median of 5 visits.

Table 5.2—Continued

Study	Treatment	Injury	Data	Sample Size	Utilization Estimates
Carey, Garett, et al. (1995)	PT and DC	Chronic low back pain	North Carolina adults with low back pain (random-digit-dialing sampling design)	269	Of those who saw a DC, mean no. of visits was 15.7. Of those who saw a PT, mean no. of visits was 17.2.
Swedlow (2005)	PT and DC	All related injuries	ICIS	610,371	From 2002 to 2004, the average no. of PT visits at 9 months after the date of injury fell from 20.4 to 11.2 visits, a 45.1% reduction, and the average number of DC manipulations recorded 9 months after injury declined from 28.5 to 12.6 visits, a 55.8% reduction.
Wasiak and McNeely (2006)	DC	Low back pain	Workers' compensation claim data from a workers' compensation carrier with a 10% share of the U.S. workers' compensation private market in 7 states	13,734	Median utilization rates varied across the 7 workers' compensation jurisdictions (Fla., Idaho, Ill., Md., N.H., N.Y., Pa.) from 5 to 14.5. Fee schedules by themselves were not associated with lower costs and utilization; however, more restrictive payment policies were associated with lower total costs per person and lower levels of service per person.
Ehrmann-Feldman et al. (1996)	PT	Back injuries	Workers' compensation claim data from Quebec, Canada	2,147	Patients who were referred to PT earlier tended to RTW faster. However, patients receiving PT tended to have longer work-duration absences than workers not receiving PT. Average was 24.5 treatments per patient.
Jette et al. (1994)	PT	Low back pain	Mail survey conducted with representatives of a national probability sample of facilities providing outpatient PT services	11,584 from 2,329 facilities	Average was 11 PT visits per episode. Found no difference between utilization in private and public facilities; however, workers' compensation claims were costlier, on average.
Mielenz et al. (1997)	PT	Acute low back pain	Telephone interview of PT practitioners in North Carolina	1,580 patients from 208 practitioners	Median PT treatments varied from 5 for patients whose first provider was an HMO and up to 7 for patients who saw a chiropractor first. Estimated mean number of treatments at 8.5.

NOTE: ICIS = Industry Claims Information System. CI = confidence interval. HMO = health maintenance organization.

mates of chiropractic utilization, Eisenberg, Kessler, et al. (1993) conducted telephone interviews in a national sample of adults and found that 10 percent of their sample had utilized chiropractic services in the previous month and the mean number of visits per user was 13.

Hurwitz, Coulter, et al. (1998) utilized data from 131 chiropractors sampled from five U.S. sites and one Canadian site and found that, of the 1,916 patients, more than 40 percent with low back pain had acute (less than three weeks) episodes, while about 20 percent had chronic (more than six months) episodes. The dominant therapeutic intervention delivered was spinal manipulative therapy, received by 80 percent of patients with low back pain. The median length of an episode for low back pain was more than twice the median length for other episodes of care (29 days versus 14 days), and there were almost twice as many visits during episodes of care for low back pain (a median of seven visits versus four visits). Their estimate of the mean number of visits for all episodes of care is 12.4, significantly higher than the median number of visits.

They noted, as did Shekelle and Brook (1991), that the large differences between the mean and median number of visits and the mean and median episode length indicate that there are long tails to the right, suggesting a small proportion of patients who are frequent or long-term users of chiropractic services causing the distribution of visits and episode length to be skewed to the right.

In a recent paper characterizing chiropractic and physical-therapy utilization in California workers' compensation claimants, Swedlow (2005) analyzed a sample of 610,371 workers' compensation claims in California that involved physical therapy or chiropractic manipulation from the Industry Claims Information System (ICIS).[2] This paper reports the average number of visits and treatment costs for claims at three, six, and nine months from the date of injury. There are dramatic changes from 2002 to the end of 2004 in both average number of visits and average amount of payments. After the implementation of the new cap on visits for physical medicine, the average number of physical-therapy visits at nine months after the date of injury fell from 20.4 to 11.2, a 45.1-percent reduction. The average number of chiropractic manipulations recorded nine months after injury also declined, from 28.5 to 12.6 visits, a 55.8-percent reduction.

There are corresponding significant decreases in average payments per claim as well. While the reductions in visits and costs are not surprising given the cap, the precap averages are quite high compared to other estimates of utilization rates. The postcap averages are more in line with the estimates provided by Shekelle and Brook (1991); Shekelle, Markovich, and Louie (1995a); Eisenberg, Kessler, et al. (1993); and Hurwitz, Coulter, et al. (1998).

In another study utilizing workers' compensation data, Wasiak and McNeely (2006) find that utilization and costs of chiropractic care vary significantly across workers' compensation jurisdictions. They report median chiropractic-care utilization rates ranging from five to 14.5 across seven workers' compensation jurisdictions (Florida, Idaho, Illinois, Maryland, New Hampshire, New York, and Pennsylvania). They also find that states with more restrictive payment policies have lower costs of chiropractic care for work-related low back pain and lower numbers of services per visit. However, they find no impact of medical fee schedules (a component of payment policies) or income-sharing policies on these variables. The authors also

[2] The ICIS database encompasses transaction-level data and, at the time of this study, included information on more than 3.5 million California workers' compensation claims contributed by large and midsize national regional insurers and self-insured employers for claims with dates of injury from 1993 through 2004.

note that the way in which the pattern of chiropractic care relates to duration of work disability and return to work remains largely unknown.

Two studies focus on utilization for chiropractic and PT services for chronic low back pain using samples of adults from North Carolina. In the first, Carey, Garett, et al. (1995) find that chiropractors are major providers of care for chronic low back pain and the people for whom they care are significantly less impaired than those who seek care from medical doctors. They note that the improved health status might be the result of care given by the DC, but it is also likely that the more severely disabled patients seek care from medical doctors who have the ability to prescribe medication and admit to the hospital and have ready access to medical subspecialists. Compared to Shekelle and Brook (1991), who find that the mean number of annual visits was 11.5 for visits of any cause, this study found an average of 15 but, this study was condition-specific to one of the most disabling musculoskeletal problems—chronic back pain. In a more recent study, Carey, Freburger, et al. (2009) survey 732 patients in North Carolina with low back pain and find that the mean number of visits to a DC was 20.8 and the mean number of visits to a PT was 15.6.

In studies focusing on PT utilization, Mielenz et al. (1997) use the same cohort as the Carey, Garett, et al. (1995) study and estimate the mean number of PT visits to be 8.5. They also find that patients who saw a PT for low back pain tended to have more severe conditions. Tsauo et al. (2009) provide the first study reporting the average number of treatment sessions and duration of PT for work-related MSDs in Taiwan. Overall, they estimate mean and median numbers of treatments of 7.8 and six, respectively. However, a small sample size and differences in the health care delivery system prevent us from assigning much weight to these estimates.

Other estimates of PT utilization ranged from 11 (Jette et al., 1994) to as low as six (Akpala et al., 1988). On the high side, Ehrmann-Feldman et al. (1996) report an average of 25 visits to PTs per episode of low back pain for workers' compensation claimants in Canada. They do find that patients who were referred earlier tended to return to work sooner than those who were referred later.

Based on our utilization literature review, rates for DC and PT treatments vary by type of injury, workers' compensation status, and geographic location. Rates tend to be higher for patients with chronic low back pain and workers' compensation claimants, and there is significant variation by geographic region. Estimates from nationally representative samples of DC utilization fall in the range of ten to 13 visits per year for any condition, whereas the majority of median rates range from five to seven. The median rates are significantly lower due to a small proportion of patients consuming a large majority of visits (Shekelle and Brook, 1991; Shekelle, Markovich, and Louie, 1995; Hurwitz, Coulter, et al., 1998). Studies focusing on patients with chronic low back pain reported higher averages, ranging between 15 and 21 treatments per year (Carey, Freburger, et al., 2009; Carey, Garett, et al., 1995). Physical-therapy utilization rates fall in the same general range as DC rates, with averages as low as six to a high of 15.6 for patients with chronic pain.

Studies focusing on workers' compensation claimants reported the highest utilization rates, and there was significant variation by geographic region. The highest averages reported were from California workers' compensation claimants prior to the recent reforms. Average utilization rates for DC and PT treatments were 28.5 and 20.4, respectively (Swedlow, 2005), though the postcap rates fell significantly to 16.6 and 11.2, respectively. In other words, after the implementation of the cap in California, utilization rates became more comparable to national estimates.

In other studies of workers' compensation claimants, median utilization rates ranged from five to 14.5 for DC care and as high as 25 PT visits for workers' compensation claimants in Canada. An interesting finding from these studies is that there was generally no impact of medical fee schedules found on costs. However, states with more restrictive payment policies had fewer visits and lower costs.

MEPS Analysis. To further analyze chiropractic and physical-therapy utilization, we employ MEPS.[3] MEPS is composed of a number of data files that contain a breadth of health utilization measures, including the number of visits to a particular type of doctor, as well as detailed injury and demographic information. These data allow us to estimate utilization rates for DC and PT services and compare differences for individuals with an MSD injury as identified by ICD-9 codes and by workers' compensation status.

We constructed our data set by combining the full-year consolidated and medical-condition files from the household component of MEPS for the years 2002–2007. We included all individuals who had experienced an injury with an identifiable ICD-9 code who went to a chiropractor or PT at least once. The drawbacks of using this data for our purposes are (1) the sample is done at the national level and state-specific data are not publicly available, and (2) the occupation codes do not allow us to identify firefighters specifically.[4] Nevertheless, the estimates do provide valuable information to help us evaluate average utilization rates and in determining how binding the cap on DC and PT treatments in California will be if care follows standard practices.

Table 5.3 reports utilization rates for chiropractic and physical- and occupational-therapy services from MEPS. As noted earlier, we analyzed a sample of individuals who had experienced an injury and sought care from a chiropractor or PT at least once. We averaged these utilization rates over the years 2002–2007 and report rates for the 25th, 50th, and 75th percentile. We also report averages for the entire sample of injured persons, as well as by segmenting those who experienced an injury at work, those who had an MSD injury, and those who had an MSD injury at work. Finally, we include the proportion of each group that exceeded 24 visits.

The average chiropractic rates fall in line with much of the literature using nationally representative samples, at 10.1 visits per year. For all injured persons, the 25th percentile was only two, while the median number of visits was six, and the 75th percentile was 13. This also falls in line with Shekelle and Brook (1991) and Hurwitz, Coulter, et al. (1998), who note that there is a heavy tail to the right of the distribution of visits, with a large portion of overall visits reported by a small fraction of individuals. The average number of visits for individuals who were injured at work is slightly higher than the overall average, at 10.6, but the difference is not significant.

---

[3] MEPS is a set of large-scale surveys of families and individuals, their medical providers, and employers across the United States. MEPS collects data on the specific health services that Americans use, how frequently they use them, and the cost of these services, as well as insurance and personal well-being measures. The household component collects data from a sample of families and individuals in selected communities across the United States, drawn from a nationally representative subsample of households that participated in the prior year's National Health Interview Survey. The medical-condition file is a subset of the individuals included in the full-year file and includes detailed information on specific medical conditions.

[4] MEPS does have individual data containing more detailed information on geography and occupation. Given the relatively small sample sizes at the state level, however, it is unlikely we would have had sufficient information on firefighters in California to conduct a meaningful analysis with the individual data.

Table 5.3
Medical Expenditure Panel Survey Chiropractic and Physical-Therapy Utilization Estimates

Utilization	Mean No. of Visits (2002–2007)	Percentile 25th	50th	75th	Percentage Using >24 Visits
Chiropractic care[a]					
All (2,830)	10.1	2	6	13	10.7
Workers' compensation (505)	10.5	2	5	13	10.9
MSD (1,090)	10.6	2	6	14	10.8
MSD and workers' compensation (218)	11.2	2	5.5	14	11.0
Physical and occupational therapy[b]					
All (2,692)	11.7	3	7	15	11.8
Workers' compensation (535)	14.0*	4	8	17	14.8
MSD (736)	11.2	3	7	15	10.6
MSD and workers' compensation (191)	13.1	4	8	17	15.7

NOTE: The number of observations in each group is shown in parentheses. workers' compensation represents individuals injured at work, and MSD represents individuals with a musculoskeletal disorder as identified through ICD-9 codes. T-tests to evaluate differences in mean number of visits were conducted (each mean is compared to the mean for all workers within each panel). * = significance at the 5% level or better.

[a] Reports descriptive statistics of the distribution of chiropractic visits for individuals who went to a DC at least once.

[b] Reports descriptive statistics of the distribution of physical- and occupational-therapy visits for individuals who went to a therapist at least once.

The statistics are similar for those who experienced an MSD, and the highest average and median utilization rates are for those who experienced an MSD at work. The median for this group is slightly lower than for others (5.5 versus six); however, the 75th percentile is slightly higher (14 versus 13). Next, we report the proportion of each sample that exceeded the 24 visits to a DC or PT. The proportion exceeding 24 visits is roughly 11 percent for each group, with the highest being for those who experienced a work-related injury, who represent 11.5 percent of the sample.

In the lower panel of Table 5.3, we report utilization rates for persons who suffered an injury and went to a physical or occupational therapist at least once. Interestingly, these utilization rates are higher than for chiropractic services, unlike in the literature; however, this might be because physical and occupational therapy are grouped together in MEPS. The average utilization rate for all those persons who went to a PT was 11.7, and the 25th, 50th, and 75th percentiles were 4, 7, and 15, respectively.

For those who suffered a work-related injury, the average utilization rate was significantly higher than the rate for the entire sample, at 13.6, and the 25th, 50th, and 75th percentiles were 4, 8, and 16, respectively. Not surprisingly, given these higher utilization rates, this group had the highest proportion of individuals who exceeded 24 visits, with 14.8 percent of the sample going to a PT more than 24 times. Utilization rates for individuals with an MSD and those with an MSD experienced at work are more in line with the entire sample, at 11.2, and

12.2, respectively, and not significantly different from the overall average. The proportion of individuals exceeding 24 visits for those with an MSD and those with an MSD experienced at work are 10 percent and 13 percent, respectively.

Chiropractic and Physical-Therapy Effectiveness Analysis

When reviewing studies to assess the effectiveness of chiropractic care and physical therapy, we focused on the type of care provided and the nature of the intervention, the study type and quality (e.g., randomized controlled trial [RCT] or quasi-experimental design), the sample size and data description (including injury type and demographic characteristics), outcome measures, incremental results (to help identify understand how the effectiveness of treatment varies over time and by number of treatments), and overall results. We included papers that clearly compared DC or PT to some other treatment (most commonly, compared to a placebo or treatment provided by a general practitioner, or GP) and gave preference to studies that performed RCTs and observational studies with a strong methodology. Since the cap is set at 24 visits, we also gave preference to studies that evaluated long-term care, although we were unable to find many studies evaluating the effectiveness of such extended periods of care.

Our search identified more than 5,700 papers that met our initial criteria, and we eventually narrowed these to 17 papers, which are summarized in Table 5.4. Of the 17 papers, 12 include an evaluation of physical or manual therapy,[5] and eight evaluate DC care. The primary comparison group was care provided by a GP (nine papers), and the majority of the papers we chose implemented an RCT design (12), in addition to five observational studies. The main injury type evaluated was back pain, with 13 of the 17 papers evaluating patients with some type of back pain (acute, subacute, chronic), three papers focused on patients with neck pain, one on sciatica, and one on osteoarthritis of the knee. Virtually all of the papers (15 of 17) included health outcomes; eight evaluated return-to-work outcomes; and six included cost analyses. Due to a lack of evidence, we found only two papers that evaluated long-term treatments.

Health Outcomes. The evidence on the health outcomes of patients treated by a DC or a PT is mildly positive. Most studies find that, relative to GP care, DC and PT treatments might provide additional benefits, particularly with patients experiencing back pain, but the benefits are small and not likely to be cost-effective. Relative to placebo therapies, DC and PT treatments fare much better, and patients generally show significant health improvements. Patients receiving DC care also report higher levels of treatment satisfaction.

In a widely cited paper, Cherkin, Deyo, et al. (1998) describe an RCT they conducted comparing DC and PT treatments with an educational booklet for patients with back pain. They found that there was a positive association between the number of treatments (contact with providers) and improvement of back-related symptoms. Further, they found that some outcomes for the DC and PT groups were superior to those of the booklet group; however, the differences were small, and, after adjustment, they were significant only for the bothersomeness of symptoms at four weeks and the subjects' satisfaction with care at one and four weeks. This study concludes that, given the limited benefits and high costs of DC and PT treatment, it seems unwise to refer all patients with low back pain to a DC or PT, although these results are limited because of the relatively short duration of treatment studied.

[5] Manual therapy is a specialization within physical therapy that provides comprehensive and conservative management for pain in the spine and extremities.

Table 5.4
Chiropractic and Physical-Therapy Effectiveness Studies

Study	Treatment	Injury	Study Type	Data and Sample Size	Outcome Measure(s)	Duration and No. of Treatments	Incremental Results	Results
Cherkin, Deyo, et al. (1998)	PT, DC, education booklet	Low back pain that persisted >7 days after primary care visit	RCT	321	11-point discomfort scale, level of dysfunction, RTW, and costs	One month with a maximum of 9 treatments	The DC group had a significantly lower discomfort score at 4 weeks than the booklet group ($p = 0.02$). This significance fell at 12 weeks ($p = 0.06$) and decreased more thereafter. There were no significant differences in discomfort between the PT and booklet groups. No significant differences were found in the Roland Disability scores.	DC and PT groups had similar outcomes that were marginally better than those of the minimal-intervention group. No significant differences among groups in the numbers of days of reduced activity or missed work or in recurrences of back pain.
Deyle et al. (2000)	MT, placebo	Osteoarthritis of the knee	RCT	83 patients in an outpatient physical-therapy practice of a large medical center	Distance walked in 6 minutes and the sum of the function, pain, and stiffness subscores (WOMAC™)	8 treatments over 4 weeks	At 4 weeks, average distance walked in 6 minutes by the treatment group improved by 12.3% ($p < 0.05$) and by 13.1% at 8 weeks ($p < 0.05$), whereas the placebo group did not change ($p > 0.05$). Average WOMAC scores were 51.8% lower in the treatment group at 4 weeks ($p < 0.05$) and 55.8% lower at 8 weeks ($p < 0.05$), whereas the scores were not significantly lower in the placebo group.	Patients receiving MT showed clinically significant improvements in distance walked and WOMAC scores at 4 and 8 weeks after treatment, whereas the comparison group showed no improvement.

Table 5.4—Continued

Study	Treatment	Injury	Study Type	Data and Sample Size	Outcome Measure(s)	Duration and No. of Treatments	Incremental Results	Results
Hoving et al. (2002)	MT, PT, GP	Neck pain	RCT	183 patients in an outpatient care setting in the Netherlands	Patient-reported success, physical dysfunction, pain intensity, and disability	6 MT, 12 PT, or continued GP care over 6 weeks		At 7 weeks, the success rates were 68.3% for MT, 50.8% for PT, and 35.9% for GP. MT scored consistently better than PT and continued care on most outcomes.
Pengel et al. (2007)	PT, advice, PT + advice	Subacute low back pain (>6 weeks and <3 months in duration)	RCT	259 persons at 7 university hospitals and primary care clinics in Australia and New Zealand	Primary outcomes were average pain over the past week, function, and global perceived effect at 6 weeks and 12 months.	12 PT or sham exercise sessions and 3 PT advice or sham advice sessions over 6 weeks		PT + advice had larger significant effects on all outcomes at 6 weeks (effect on pain, –1.5 points, $p = 0.001$, with similar effects for other primary outcomes). At 12 months, there was a statistically significant effect only for function (1.1 points, $p = 0.005$).
Luijsterburg et al. (2007)	PT and GP	Sciatica	RCT	135 patients in participating GP offices in Rotterdam	Global perceived effect, quality of life, direct and indirect costs, RTW	Maximum of 9 treatments or consultations in 6 weeks	The relative risk ratios of GP+PT care to GP care only at 3, 6, 12, and 52 weeks were 1.4, 1.3, 1.1, and 1.4, respectively. Patient utility at each follow-up for both groups was not statistically different.	Significant difference on perceived recovery at 1-year follow-up in favor of the PT group. No incremental effect on quality of life or statistically significant difference in days to RTW. The PT treatment is not more cost-effective than GP.

Table 5.4—Continued

Study	Treatment	Injury	Study Type	Data and Sample Size	Outcome Measure(s)	Duration and No. of Treatments	Incremental Results	Results
Niemistö et al. (2005)	MT + stabilizing + GP, GP	Chronic low back pain (Oswestry Disability Index >15%)	RCT	204	Pain, disability, health-related quality of life, satisfaction with care, and costs	4 sessions of MT + stabilizing exercises	Significant improvement occurred in both groups. The treatment group showed a slightly more significant reduction in pain ($p = 0.01$) and had a significantly higher patient satisfaction ($p = 0.001$).	GP alone was more cost-effective for both health care use and work absenteeism and led to equal improvement in disability and health-related quality of life.
Hurwitz, Morgenstern, Harber, et al. (2002)	GP, GP + PT, DC (with and without physical modalities)	Low back pain	RCT	681 participants in a large managed care facility from 1995 to 1998	Average and most severe low back pain intensity in the past week and low back–related disability	From baseline to 6 months, mean DC visits were 5.7(3.3) with a range of 0–21 and median of 5. For the GP+PT group, the mean was 5.4(4.6) with a range of 1–21 and median of 4.	Mean differences in most severe pain, average pain, and disability score were measured at 0–2-week, 0–6-week, and 0–6-month intervals. Most differences were statistically insignificant; however, there was a significant improvement in disability for PT patients compared to GP.	After 6 months of follow-up, DC and GP for low back pain were comparable in their effectiveness. PT is marginally more effective than GP for reducing disability, but the possible benefit is small.
Goldby et al. (2006)	PT (manual therapy or spinal stabilization), minimal intervention	Chronic low back pain (current episode >12 weeks)	RCT	346	Intensity of low back pain, disability, handicap, medication, and quality of life	A maximum of 10 spinal-stabilization treatments, 10 MT interventions, or an education booklet	Significant benefits of spinal manipulation in pain reduction at 6 mo. ($p = 0.009$); however, this benefit was not significant at 12 months.	The spinal-stabilization group experienced a significant reduction in Oswestry Disability Index scores (38.8%) ($p = 0.025$).

Table 5.4—Continued

Study	Treatment	Injury	Study Type	Data and Sample Size	Outcome Measure(s)	Duration and No. of Treatments	Incremental Results	Results
Torstensen et al. (1998)	Medical exercise therapy, PT, and self-exercise by walking	Chronic low back pain or radicular pain (>8 wks <52 wks)	RCT	208	Pain intensity, functional ability, patient satisfaction, RTW, number of days on sick leave, and costs	36 treatments over 3 months	No difference was observed between the medical exercise therapy and PT groups, but both were significantly better than the self-exercise group. Patient satisfaction was highest for medical exercise. RTW rates were equal for all 3 groups 15 months after the therapy started.	RTW rates were similar for the 3 groups. The PT groups had fewer days on sick leave than the self-exercise group during the treatment and follow-up period. PT groups were cost-effective.
Carey, Garett, et al. (1995)	GP (HMO & primary care), DC, orthopedic surgeons	Acute low back pain	Observational	1,633 patients enrolled with 286 practitioners in North Carolina	Use of health care services, functional status, costs, and RTW	Patients visiting a DC had the highest number of visits (13.2 for urban and 9.0 for rural) compared to visits to other providers ($p < 0.001$).	Within 25 days after initial visit, the proportion of patients with functional impairment reduced from almost 100% to roughly 20%, but there were no significant differences between the groups.	Time to functional recovery, RTW, and complete recovery from low back pain were similar for all groups. Mean total estimated outpatient charges were highest for orthopedic surgeons and DCs. Satisfaction was greatest among the DC group.

Table 5.4—Continued

Study	Treatment	Injury	Study Type	Data and Sample Size	Outcome Measure(s)	Duration and No. of Treatments	Incremental Results	Results
Wasiak, Kim, and Pransky (2007)	DC initiated and concluded within 30 days of beginning of episode, DC initiated within 30 days but not concluded within 30 days, DC initiated more than 30 days from beginning	Work-related low back pain	Observational	6,019 patients from a workers' compensation carrier with a 10% share of the U.S. private market (Fla., Ill., N.H., Pa.)	RTW	Mean(SD) visits for the entire sample was 15.5(20.1). Mean for all cases and those with lost work time for each group are 5.5(5.9) and 7.1(7.9) for group 1, 23.4(21.3) and 28.4(25.8) for group 2, and 21.0(30.3) and 23.8(35.6) for group 3.		DC was initiated within 30 days after the onset of occupational lower back pain by 89% of claimants. Of those claimants, 48% ended DC within the first 30 days. Shorter DC duration was significantly associated with a lower likelihood of work-disability recurrence (odds ratio = 0.39) and 8.6% shorter work-disability duration.
Haas et al. (2004)	DC, GP	Acute and chronic ambulatory low back pain	Observational	2,870 from 51 DC and 14 GP community clinics	Pain and functional disability		Pain and disability scores were significantly better for DC patients at 2 weeks as well as 1-, 3-, 6-, and 12-month measurements ($p < 0.001$). No significant differences were observed at 24-, 36-, or 48-month follow-ups.	DC patients experienced significantly better outcomes in pain and disability, but most improvement was seen by 3 months and sustained for 1 year; any advantages were insignificant thereafter.

Table 5.4—Continued

Study	Treatment	Injury	Study Type	Data and Sample Size	Outcome Measure(s)	Duration and No. of Treatments	Incremental Results	Results
Walker et al. (2008)	MT, minimal intervention	Neck pain	RCT	94 patients referred to 3 physical-therapy clinics	Neck disability indexes, pain visual analog scales, patient-perceived global rating of change, treatment success rates, and post-treatment health care utilization	Twice weekly for up to 3 weeks	Both groups experienced significant decreases in neck pain disability index, cervical VAS pain scores, and upper-extremity VAS pain scores from baseline to 1 year measured at 3 weeks, 6 weeks, and 1 year. The MT group mean was significantly lower for the neck pain index at each measurement and cervical VAS at 3 and 6 weeks but not significant one year after treatment. 62% of therapy and 32% of intervention patients perceived treatment success ($p = 0.004$).	Significant improvements were found in short-term pain, disability, and patient-perceived recovery with the use of MT for mechanical neck pain.
Zigenfus et al. (2000)	PT started at either the day of or first day after injury, 2–7 days after injury, or >7 days after injury.	Acute low back pain	Observational	3,867 patients randomly selected from the database of a large occupational health care provider	Physician visits, case duration, duration of restricted work, and days away from work	Average number of treatments for the early treatment group was 3.1 and significantly lower than both other groups.		The early-intervention group had significantly fewer treatments, fewer restricted workdays, fewer days away from work, and shorter case duration than the other groups.

Table 5.4—Continued

Study	Treatment	Injury	Study Type	Data and Sample Size	Outcome Measure(s)	Duration and No. of Treatments	Incremental Results	Results
Koes et al. (1992)	MT, PT, GP	Back and neck complaints (>6 weeks)	RCT	256	Severity of main complaint, global perceived effect, pain, and functional status	3 months; no. of treatments is unclear.	Statistically significant improvement of the main complaint at 3 weeks for those treated with MT compared to GP and a significant improvement for those treated with PT compared to GP. There were no significant differences at 12 weeks. Differences in global perceived effects were significant between MT and GP and between PT and GP at each interval up to 12 weeks.	PT and MT decreased the severity of complaints and had a higher global perceived effect compared to GP. There were no significant differences between MT and PT.
Meade et al. (1990)	DC, GP	low back pain	RCT	741	Oswestry pain, disability, results of tests of straight leg raising and lumbar flexion	Maximum of 10 DC treatments over 3 months (but might be extended to 1 year). Mean(SD) for DC group was 9.1(3.6) and for GP was 6.3(4.8). Mean difference is significant ($p < 0.001$).	Differences in changes in Oswestry score between DC and GP groups were not significant at 6 weeks, were marginally significant at 6 months (3% difference, $p < 0.05$), not significant at 1 year, and significant at 2 years (7%, $p < 0.01$).	Marginally beneficial effects of DC compared to GP in patients with low back pain.

Table 5.4—Continued

Study	Treatment	Injury	Study Type	Data and Sample Size	Outcome Measure(s)	Duration and No. of Treatments	Incremental Results	Results
W. Johnson, Baldwin, and Butler (1999)	DC, GP	Back pain	Observational	850	Costs, patterns of care, and RTW	Mean nos. of office visits for medical only, temporary, and PPD cases for GP are 4.6, 5.2, and 5.9, respectively. For DC, means are 11.4, 11.5, and 11.5, respectively.		Controlling for unobserved heterogeneity between DC and GP groups yields insignificant differences in outcomes between patients treated by DC or GP.
Shekelle, Markovich, and Louie (1995)	DC, PT, GP	Back pain	Observational	686	Costs, utilization			Chiropractors have significantly greater mean number of visits per episode than other providers. DC had the highest mean outpatient cost per episode, and GP had the lowest.
M. R. Johnson, Schultz, and Ferguson (1989)	DC, GP, OP	Work-related sprains and strains	Observational	862	Costs, RTW			Find that those who received DC care had fewer lost workdays. Median provider cost was highest for DC; mean was highest for GP.

As part of the University of California, Los Angeles (UCLA) low back pain study, Hurwitz, Morgenstern, Harber, et al. (2002) performed an RCT on 681 patients who were assigned to medical care (GP), medical care with physical therapy, or chiropractic care. They found that DC and GP treatments were comparable for low back pain in their effectiveness after six months of follow-up and that PT was marginally more effective than GP for reducing disability, but the possible benefit is small. In an 18-month follow-up with the same group, Hurwitz, Morgenstern, Kominski, et al. (2006) found no differences in outcomes between medical and chiropractic care, although chiropractic care might result in a greater likelihood of perceived improvement. They do find that physical therapy might be more effective than medical care alone for some patients.

Other studies focusing on low back pain find mildly positive results for DC and PT treatments. Pengel et al. (2007) find that physiotherapist-directed exercise and advice are more effective in treating patients with subacute low back pain than the placebo treatment of exercises and advice. Their effect is significant at six weeks but diminish 12 months after treatment. Goldby et al. (2006) follows subjects with chronic back pain in a spinal-stabilization rehabilitation group, manual therapy, or a minimal-intervention group. The authors find significant improvements in the spinal-stabilization group, but only reductions in Oswestry Disability Index and medication use are significant after 12 months. They note that spinal stabilization appears to be more effective than manual therapy, which is, in turn, more effective than a simple education booklet.

Koes et al. (1992) finds a decrease in severity of complaints for patients treated with PT; however, the authors note that a substantial part of the effect appeared to be due to nonspecific (placebo) effects. Finally, in a nonrandomized observational study, Haas et al. (2004) finds that most improvement with DC treatment was seen by three months after treatment and that the benefits were usually sustained for up to a year; however, exacerbation was seen thereafter.

Additional studies evaluated treatments for osteoarthritis and neck pain. Deyle et al. (2000) finds significant impacts of manual therapy on patients with osteoarthritis of the knee; however, there is no cost-effectiveness analysis to compare the benefits of the treatment with the costs. Hoving et al. (2002) examines manual therapy performed by physical therapists and finds improved outcomes for patients with neck pain over a seven-week duration compared to patients receiving GP care. Finally, in a comparison of manual therapy and a minimal intervention, Walker et al. (2008) finds that manual therapy is more effective in reducing pain, reducing disability, and increasing perceived treatment success in patients with mechanical neck pain.

We also reviewed two recent meta-analyses that evaluate spinal manipulation, one of the most common treatments provided by chiropractors. Cherkin et al. (2002) reviews 26 RCTs evaluating spinal manipulation for acute and chronic back pain and reports that manipulation was superior to sham therapies and therapies judged to have no evidence of a benefit but was not superior to effective conventional treatments. Further, Assendelft et al. (2003) performs a metaregression analysis of 39 RCTs and finds that spinal manipulation is superior to other forms of treatment for acute or chronic low back pain only when compared with sham therapies or therapies known to be ineffective, such as traction or bed rest.

Return to Work and Cost-Effectiveness. The evidence on RTW outcomes and cost for injured workers utilizing DC or PT treatments is mixed. Most studies do not find a significant effect on RTW rates and find that DC and PT treatments are not be as cost-effective as more conventional therapies administered by a GP. However, there is one paper that does address long-term treatment and finds a positive cost-effectiveness for PT. Three of the papers evaluating RTW or cost implement an RCT design, whereas four papers are observational studies.

In one of the only long-term treatment studies, Torstensen et al. (1998) evaluated 208 injured persons in Norway with chronic low back pain. The treatment group in this study received 36 treatments of one of two types of physiotherapy: conventional physiotherapy or medical exercise therapy. The control group underwent self-exercise therapy. The authors find significant improvements for the patients in the physiotherapy group compared to the self-exercise group, but they do not find any difference in return-to-work rates between the groups. However, they do note that the two PT groups recorded fewer sick-leave days during treatment. After incorporating this into the cost-benefit analysis, they find that both PT groups had lower costs than the self-exercise group. While this is one of the few studies that evaluate long-term treatment, we do have to be wary of comparing results from different health care systems.

Two additional RCT studies evaluate the cost-effectiveness of PT and DC treatments. Niemistö et al. (2005) finds that combined manipulative treatment, stabilizing exercises, and physician consultation did not yield more cost-effective outcomes than physician consultation alone. This study finds that consultation alone was more cost-effective for both health care use and work absenteeism and led to equal improvement in disability and health-related quality of life. However, the number of treatments was small. In another study, Luijsterburg et al. (2007) evaluated 135 patients with sciatica in the Netherlands and compared the effects of nine PT and GP treatments on a number of outcomes. While the authors did find a significant difference on perceived recovery at the one-year follow-up in favor of the PT group, they found no incremental effect on quality of life or a statistically significant difference in days to RTW. Furthermore, they conclude that the PT treatment is not more cost-effective than GP.

In an observational study evaluating cost-effectiveness and return to work, Carey, Garett, et al. (1995) finds no significant difference in time to functional recovery, return to work, or complete recovery from low back pain based on six provider types (orthopedic surgeon, HMO, primary care rural, primary care urban, chiropractic urban, and chiropractic rural). The study does find significantly higher costs for chiropractic services and higher utilization than other provider types; however, there is greater satisfaction reported for patients seen by chiropractors.

William Johnson, Baldwin, and Butler (1999) estimate differences in costs, outcomes, and RTW between patients treated by a DC and those treated by a GP. They find that costs for an average work-related back claim are lower for DC patients than for GP patients because more DC patients RTW within the three-day waiting period, and those with temporary-disability claims RTW more quickly. However, once they control for unobserved heterogeneity between the groups, the significance disappears. They say that this might be because DC treatment returns injured workers to their jobs more quickly by providing continuing care after workers return. Another explanation they posit is that chiropractors treat less severe back injuries, on average, than do physicians. In an earlier study focusing on work-related sprains and strains, M. R. Johnson, Schultz, and Ferguson (1989) compare chiropractic, medical, and osteopathic care. They find that claimants who saw chiropractors lost one less day of work, on average, than claimants who saw other practitioners (eight compared with nine days of work lost). However, only one-third of claimants responded to the survey, and no adjustments were made for baseline demographic characteristics or clinical severity. In addition, claimants selected providers themselves.

Wasiak, Kim, and Pransky (2007) used workers' compensation claim data from four states that cover 10 percent of the private market to analyze outcomes of workers who experienced occupational low back pain and saw a chiropractor at least once. They analyzed utilization and return-to-work outcomes and found that, after controlling for multiple factors, shorter chiropractic-care duration was significantly associated with a lower likelihood of work-disability recurrence (odds ratio = 0.39) and 8.6-percent shorter work-disability duration. Workers initiating and concluding chiropractic care shortly after an injury had significantly fewer chiropractic visits and a lower share of DC visits in overall utilization than those who delayed treatment. However, as the authors note, there are limitations in interpreting their results because it is not possible to determine whether more DC care leads to more work disability or whether work disability leads to more DC care. In particular, this study was not able to include any measure of severity of back-pain conditions, although the authors did create a cohort similar to those used in previous studies of uncomplicated low back pain in workers' compensation sets.

Zigenfus et al. (2000) also evaluate cost-effectiveness and return to work while studying the effects of initiating early physical-therapy treatment. They find that workers receiving treatment either the day of injury or the day after experienced significantly fewer physician visits, fewer restricted workdays, fewer days away from work, and shorter case duration than the other groups. This conclusion assumes that initiating early physical therapy has a causal effect of improving outcomes, but there may be underlying differences in the groups examined (e.g., injury severity, unobservable characteristics) that explain the differences in outcomes. However, this study found no significant differences among the three groups in injury severity, which does improve the credibility of the results.

In a study focusing on treatment costs, Shekelle, Markovich, and Louie (1995a) compared the costs between provider types of episodes of back-pain care. Analyzing RAND Health Insurance Experiment data, they find that chiropractors served as the primary providers for 40 percent of the back-pain episodes and had the highest mean outpatient costs. Although chiropractors charged less each episode than other practitioners did, they saw patients an average of 10.4 times per episode, approximately twice as often as any other type of provider. GPs saw their patients only 2.3 times per episode and had the lowest mean outpatient and overall costs. Finally, in a recent review of cost-effectiveness studies of medical and chiropractic care for occupational low back pain, Baldwin et al. (2001) find that chiropractors and physicians provide equally effective care for occupational low back pain but that chiropractic patients are more satisfied with their care. Furthermore, they report that evidence on relative costs of medical and chiropractic care is conflicting.

Summary

We evaluated the utilization and effectiveness of DC and PT treatments in this section. From our review of the literature and analysis of MEPS, we find that average utilization rates were ten to 14 visits for most conditions, with slightly higher averages for patients with chronic low back pain and for workers' compensation claimants. These estimates fall in line with ACOEM recommendations of roughly seven to 12 visits to a DC or PT per injury episode. We also find a large difference in mean and median rates, indicating that there is a skewed distribution of visits. The highest utilization rates were for workers' compensation claimants in California prior to the recent reforms; however, since the reforms, utilization rates have fallen more in line with national averages. Furthermore, from our analysis of MEPS, we find that roughly 10 percent of individuals who seek DC or PT treatment will go more than 24 times.

We also assessed existing studies that evaluated the effectiveness of DC and PT treatments with respect to health outcomes, RTW, and cost-effectiveness. Most studies evaluating the health effects of DC and PT treatments find mildly positive results relative to GP care and significant improvements relative to placebos. The evidence regarding return-to-work outcomes and cost-effectiveness was mixed and weak. While some studies do find that DC and PT treatments are marginally cost-effective and return injured workers to work faster, they are sparse, and many studies find that alternative treatments from a GP are more cost-effective. However, there is still a lack of evidence on long-term treatments.

From our findings, we can draw some conclusions as to the overall impact on firefighter outcomes of the recent cap on DC and PT treatments. ACOEM guidelines suggest that virtually all injury conditions treated by a DC or PT can be treated well within the new 24-treatment cap, and our utilization estimates confirm that most individuals do not require that much treatment. However, given the higher injury risks firefighters face, it still might be the case that many would otherwise want treatment levels beyond the 24-visit cap.

Given this, what does the literature suggest about the potential effect of the cap on firefighters who are denied the additional treatment? Based on our review of the effectiveness of DC and PT treatments, it does not appear that outcomes will dramatically worsen. DC and PT treatment does not appear to be correlated with significantly better health, RTW, or cost-effectiveness outcomes for injured workers than treatment from a GP. There is also no evidence that the firefighters would experience differential effects of treatment. That said, some of this lack of evidence is due to limitations in the existing evidence base.

In the next section, we examine the employment outcomes of firefighters before and after the cap. This analysis provides additional input into the overall effects of limiting DC and PT treatments for injured firefighters.

Empirical Analysis of the Impact of the Medical Reforms

Here, we conduct our own analysis of the impact of the reforms to medical treatment on the employment outcomes of firefighters with MSDs. The reforms introduced by SB 228 and SB 899 led to significant reductions in the utilization of medical treatment, particularly the use of chiropractic care and physical therapy, for workers' compensation cases in California. We do not have the data to identify those patients who utilize DC or PT therapy and to test the impact of the reforms specifically on them. But, given the large impact of the reforms on utilization, if we thought that patients were being denied access to necessary care that had a truly beneficial impact on outcomes, then we would expect to observe a worsening of outcomes for patients on average after the adoption of the reforms.

Analysis of Trends

In this analysis, we use the matched data on permanent-disability ratings from the DEU and earnings from the EDD that we described in Chapter Three. We use the same sample, combining data on firefighters with data on police officers, corrections officers, teachers, construction workers, and laborers. We measure outcomes in terms of employment and lost wages relative to the matched uninjured control workers. Specifically, we focus on employment outcomes two years after injury—that is, whether the worker is employed and how much he or she earns in the eighth quarter after injury. We focus on outcomes two years after injury because two years is the latest period for which we have earnings data for all workers injured through 2006 in the sample, and it is long enough for some of the special provisions offered to public-safety employees (and, to a lesser extent, teachers) to have been exhausted.

We first present a simple descriptive analysis that compares the relative employment ratio and earnings losses of workers over time by year of injury. The medical reforms took effect on January 1, 2004. Specifically, the utilization review and medical treatment guidelines were applied to all treatment rendered on or after January 1, 2004, and the 24-visit cap applied to all injuries after that date. If these reforms had a significant impact on the employment outcomes of injured workers, then we would expect to see a worsening of outcomes for workers injured in 2004 or later. If we do not see such an effect, it suggests either that the reforms did not have an adverse effect on outcomes or that the effect was small enough on average to be offset by other factors.

Figure 5.1 illustrates the trends in employment by occupation from 2004 to 2006 (2007 is dropped because we do not have two full years of postinjury outcomes for all workers). The vertical axis in each panel reports the relative employment ratio, and the horizontal axis reports the year of injury. We are looking at the relative employment two years after injury, meaning that, for workers injured in, say, 2004, we are examining their employment outcomes in 2006. In terms of evaluating the impact of the reforms, we are testing whether changes to treatment received in the first two years after injury have any perceptible impact on the likelihood that a disabled worker has returned and is still working in year 2.

Figure 5.1
Relative Employment Ratios Two Years After Injury, by Occupation and Year of Injury

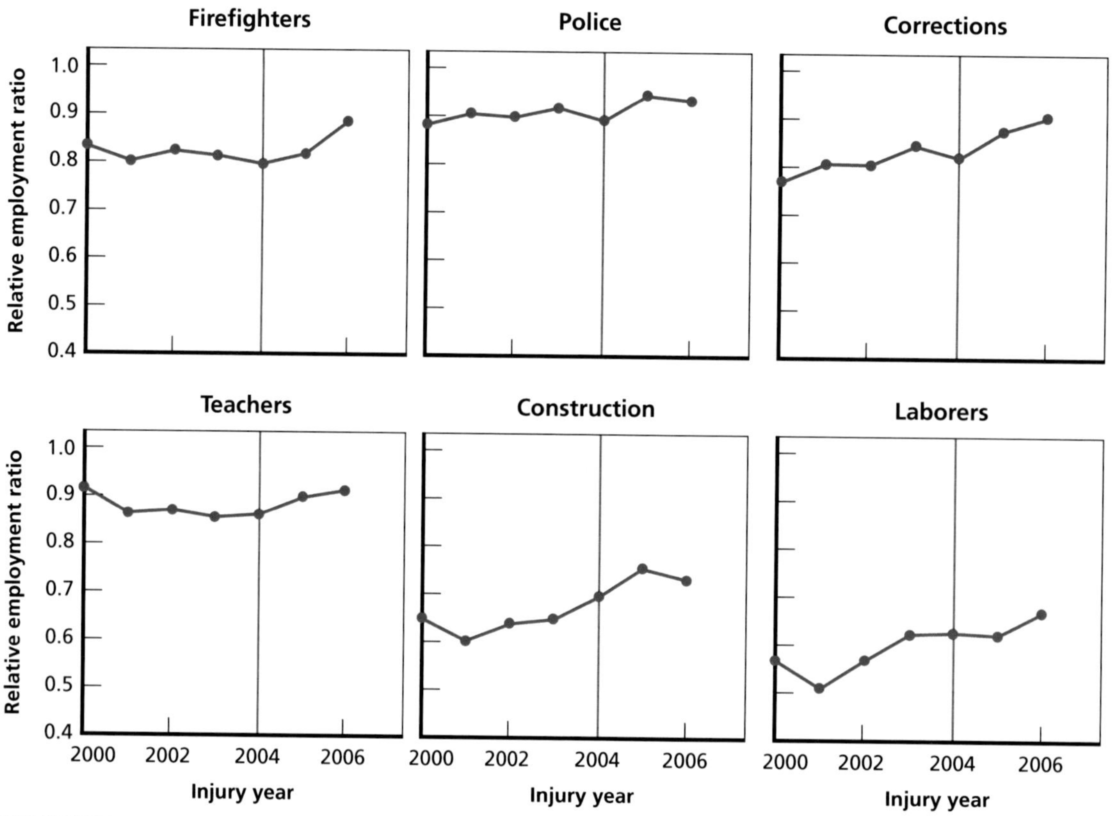

RAND *MG1018-5.1*

In general, the figure offers little to suggest that the reforms led to a significant decline in outcomes for injured workers. There appears to be a slight drop in 2004 relative to 2003 for firefighters, police, and corrections. This finding is not consistent across the full set of occupations, however, and outcomes in most occupations are better for workers injured in 2005.

It is likely that the medical reforms had a differential impact on certain types of injuries, particularly MSDs. This is certainly true of the caps on chiropractic care and physical therapy, which disproportionately affect workers with spinal injuries. Even absent the caps, however, we expect that the use of treatment guidelines likely led to a reduction in these kinds of treatments. Nuckols et al. (2005) evaluated many sets of treatment guidelines and generally found the clinical content to be insufficient in the use of chiropractic care and physical therapy for common musculoskeletal conditions.

Figure 5.2 reports the trends in relative employment ratios for firefighters with back, shoulder, and knee injuries from 2000 through 2006. The vertical axis reports the average relative employment ratio for each injury type, and the horizontal axis reports the year of injury. As before, the relative employment reported refers to two years after injury (quarter 8).

Again, the figure offers little to suggest that the medical reforms had a negative effect on the employment outcomes of disabled firefighters. There is a drop from 2004 to 2005 and 2006 for knee injuries. But the trends for back injuries and shoulder injuries, which we expect were affected by the reforms more strongly than knee injuries, suggest a general improvement in employment outcomes since the reforms.

Taken together, these figures offer little support for the fear that the medical reforms led to significantly worse outcomes for firefighters, with or without musculoskeletal injuries. The only observed trend in employment over this period appears to be positive. While certainly not conclusive, these results suggest either that the reforms had little impact on employment outcomes or that the effects were small enough that they were offset by other factors.

Figure 5.2
Relative Employment Ratios Two Years After Injury, by Injury Type and Year of Injury, Firefighters Only

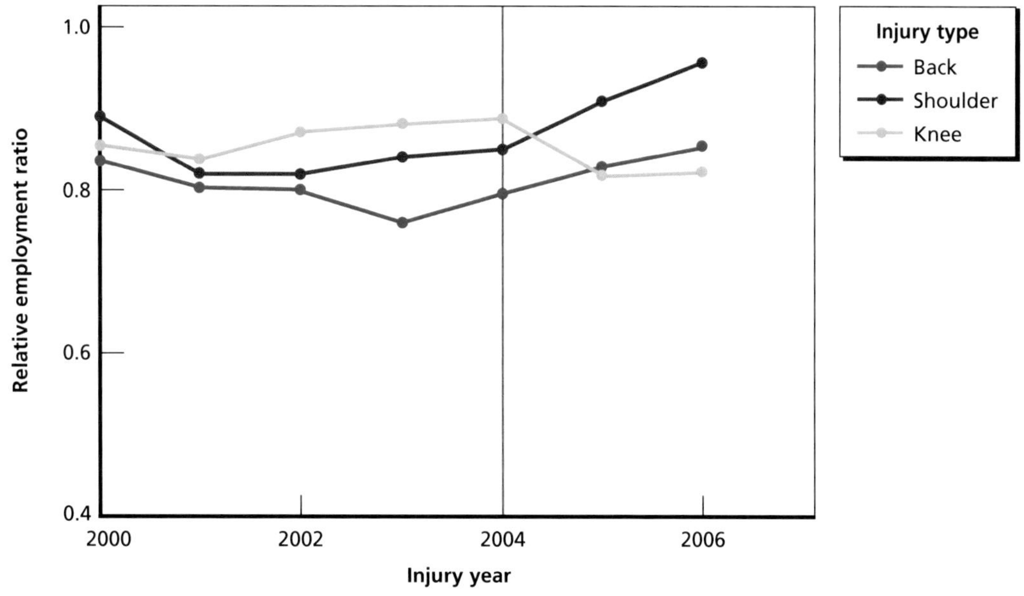

RAND *MG1018-5.2*

A Statistical Model

While the descriptive analysis is suggestive, there are a number of potentially confounding factors that could affect return to work that are not controlled for by simply analyzing trends. There could be changes in the characteristics of disabled workers, such as the average age or the type or severity of injuries they experience. Underlying economic trends could affect the demand for labor and influence the likelihood that a disabled worker is able to find a job. If any of these changes coincides with the adoption of the medical treatment reforms, then it will compromise our ability to draw conclusions from observed changes in return to work.

In an attempt to control for these confounding factors, we employ a statistical model that isolates the impact of the reforms from those of these other factors. Specifically, we estimate a series of multivariate regression models that estimate the likelihood that the injured worker has positive earnings in the eighth quarter after injury as a function of other characteristics of individuals. These include age at the date of injury, the severity of the injury, preinjury wages, and the average fraction of uninjured control workers who are working.[6] A natural measure of injury severity is the actual disability rating in the DEU. Given the changes that we know are occurring over this period, as described in Chapter Four, we adopt an alternative measure. We create a series of dummy variables indicating the quintiles of disability ratings within a year and use these dummy variables to capture severity (so, for example, the top dummy variable indicates that the injury was rated in the top quintile of injuries in the year).

Because we are attempting to capture the impact of the reform, it is important that we control for confounding time trends. We use a quadratic specification of the quarter of injury and test for a discrete change at the date that the reforms became effective (i.e., the start of 2004). To check the variability of our findings, we test separately for an effect among all workers and among firefighters. Within these groups, we also test separately for an effect on workers with back injuries, shoulder injuries, or knee injuries. For firefighters, we also test for an effect on workers with heart disease.

Even after controlling for the other variables in our regression model, there could be other underlying trends that affect the employment outcomes of workers throughout the workers' compensation system. In order to weed out such trends, we adopt an alternative specification that compares the outcomes of an injury type we think was especially affected by the reforms to a set of injuries that we think should have been largely unaffected. Specifically, we compare workers with back injuries to a "control" group comprised of workers with impaired vision, impaired hearing, lung disease, heart disease, psychiatric disabilities, or post-traumatic head syndrome. It seems unlikely that the medical care provided to workers with any of this latter set of injuries would have been significantly affected by the introduction of treatment guidelines, at least not to the extent that those with back injuries were. Conceptually, we can think of this approach as a "difference-in-differences" estimate that separates out the impact of the reform specifically on back injuries from those trends common to all workers' compensation claims. Because some of these are not generally considered occupational for other occupations, we restrict this analysis to firefighters.

The results of our statistical analysis are reported in Table 5.5. The table reports the estimated impact of the cap, the standard error of the estimate, and the *p*-value indicating the sta-

[6] The employment of individuals and their controls have a large number of zeros, so the relative employment ratio is too volatile to compute at the individual level. Thus, we use the overall level of employment as the dependent variable and control for the employment of control workers as a dependent variable.

Table 5.5
Estimates from a Statistical Model of the Impact of the Medical Reforms on Employment Outcomes for Disabled Workers: Dependent Variable Is Likelihood of Working Two Years After Injury

Injured	Estimated Impact of Reforms	Standard Error	*p*-Value
All workers			
All injuries	−0.03	0.01	0.01
Back injuries	−0.03	0.02	0.11
Shoulder injuries	−0.05	0.03	0.18
Knee injuries	−0.02	0.02	0.44
Firefighters			
All injuries	0.02	0.03	0.52
Back injuries	0.02	0.05	0.75
Shoulder injuries	0.03	0.07	0.70
Knee injuries	0.03	0.04	0.43
Heart disease	−0.15	0.20	0.46
Back injuries versus other injuries	−0.09	0.07	0.20

NOTE: The table reports the estimated effect of the medical reforms on the relative employment ratio of workers in the eighth quarter after injury.

tistical significance of the findings. The standard errors are computed using the Huber-White "robust" variance estimation method. In order to be considered statistically significant at conventional levels, the *p*-value must be at or below at least 0.1 and typically below 0.05.

The table provides little support for the idea that the reforms had a significant negative impact on employment outcomes for injured workers, and essentially no evidence of an effect on firefighters. The only coefficient that is statistically significant at conventional levels is the first estimate—the impact of the reforms on all workers for all injuries. The effect suggests a reduction of −0.03 to the relative employment ratio. The average employment level in quarter 8 of workers in our sample is 0.62, so this represents a reduction in the likelihood of working of about 4.8 percent.

While this is suggestive of an effect, we find little support in our other estimates. The impact on back injuries, which we expect to have been affected most by the reforms, has the same magnitude (a reduction of 0.03), but it is not statistically significant at even the 10-percent level. The impact on shoulder injuries is larger in magnitude, and the effect on knee injuries is smaller in magnitude, but neither of these effects is statistically significant.

Whatever impact we find overall, there appears to be none on firefighters. The coefficient estimate actually suggests that the reforms led to a 0.02 increase in postinjury employment of firefighters, though the estimate is highly imprecise and not even close to being statistically significant at any conventional level. In fact, all of the individual coefficients on firefighters are positive except for the estimate on heart disease, which is negative and relatively large at −0.15, though also not significant. The positive sign on these coefficients is meaningful, because it suggests that the lack of a finding for firefighters cannot be entirely explained by a lack of statistical power due to smaller samples. If that were the case, we would still expect to find a negative coefficient.

The final row of the table reports our difference-in-differences estimate comparing back injuries to other injuries. Here, we find a negative effect of –0.09, which is fairly large (the baseline employment rate in quarter 8 for this sample is 0.76, suggesting about a 12-percent difference). But, as with most of the other estimates, the effect is not statistically significant. This finding could possibly be attributed to a lack of power, but our sample for this group is 1,365, which is not trivial for a simple regression model like this.

Summary

Overall, our empirical analysis finds little support for the notion that the adoption of the medical treatment reforms had an adverse impact on the employment outcomes of firefighters, with or without MSDs. This does not necessarily mean that the reforms had no effect. It simply means we could find no evidence of an effect, either because there was no effect or because the effect was small enough—or centered in a small enough subset of the population—that it did not affect the average outcome of workers studied here. There was a small hint of a negative effect for workers overall, but even this was not robust across different injury types.

CHAPTER SIX

Conclusions

This study examined the frequency and severity of work-related MSDs experienced by firefighters in California. We compared the average risk of firefighters to that of other occupations; we evaluated the impact of injuries on the employment outcomes for firefighters; and we studied how firefighters with MSDs were affected by recent reforms to the disability rating system and medical delivery system in California. Here, we summarize our key findings and discuss the implications for policy and for future research.

Unsurprisingly, our study finds that firefighters are subject to considerably more risk of nonfatal injuries than workers in the private sector. This includes both musculoskeletal and other kinds of injuries, but it is more pronounced for MSDs. In particular, firefighters 55 and older are more than ten times more likely to suffer an MSD than are private-sector workers of the same age, and, when injured, these older firefighters take more than four times longer to return to work.

While the frequency and severity of MSDs is greater for firefighters, our analysis suggests that this does not necessarily translate into worse long-term economic consequences for workers. While firefighters have worse employment and earnings after an injury than some other public employees (such as teachers), their employment and earnings are considerably better than those for private-sector workers in physically demanding jobs (such as construction workers). Firefighters 55 and older, however, do appear to suffer comparable long-term earning and employment losses comparable to those of private-sector workers the same age. Nevertheless, given the availability of special compensation packages to these employees, such as disability retirement benefits, it is likely that the overall economic impact is less severe for firefighters than for private-sector workers on average.

We also find that firefighters experienced significant declines in average permanent-disability ratings as a result of the reforms to the disability rating system. The declines experienced by firefighters are comparable to those experienced by other workers. Somewhat unexpectedly, however, the biggest impact on firefighters appears to have come from a disproportionately large fraction of cases that now receive a zero disability rating. Our data do not allow us to say for sure whether these zero ratings are, in fact, for musculoskeletal conditions. Given the physical demands of the job, however, it seems possible that firefighters were more likely under the old system than under the new system to receive a disability rating based on a physician's assessment of work restrictions under the old system.

If this explanation is accurate, then it would suggest that the efforts to reduce subjectivity in the disability rating system have had a disproportionate impact on firefighters. We do note, however, that our findings suggest that those workers who receive zero ratings also tend to exhibit very little earning losses associated with their injury. In this sense, it suggests that the zero ratings in the new system are affecting mostly minor cases with little impairment for workers, at least on average.

The final part of our study examines whether firefighters were adversely affected by the adoption of provisions designed to curb the utilization of certain types of medical treatment. Our review of the existing clinical evidence provides little support for the idea that utilization review should have a substantially negative impact on outcomes for injured workers. We find relatively few studies that document a substantial benefit of chiropractic care or physical therapy on employment or health outcomes for injured workers relative to conventional physician treatments. We do note, however, that the existing literature tends to focus on much less intensive levels of treatment (that is, fewer visits per injury) than was seen in California's workers' compensation system prior to the reforms. While, on the one hand, that suggests that the levels of utilization in California's system exceeded standard practice, it makes it difficult to apply the existing literature to assess whether we would expect the reforms to affect worker outcomes.

Our own empirical analysis finds little evidence that firefighters were adversely affected by the reforms. We compared firefighter outcomes before and after the reforms. We also compared firefighters with injuries that were more likely to be affected to those with injuries that were less likely to be affected, in order to better control for other possible factors influencing employment outcomes. None of these analyses suggested that the employment outcomes of firefighters were worse after the adoption of the medical reforms.

It can be challenging to draw meaningful policy implications from a null result such as this. We feel that it is important to stress that our findings do not mean that the medical reforms had no effect. Rather, our findings suggest that any effect on firefighters was either too small in the average worker for us to detect or that it was offset by other changes in the economy or the workers' compensation system. Whether the reforms had a more significant impact on workers in other occupations is unclear, though we feel that it is a subject worthy of further research.

APPENDIX

Multivariate Analysis

To supplement our descriptive analysis and attempt to identify the impact of reforms while controlling for other confounding factors, we employ a statistical model isolating the impact of the reforms independent of other factors. Specifically, we estimate a series of multivariate regression models that estimate the likelihood that the injured worker has positive earnings in the eighth quarter after injury as a function of other characteristics of individuals.

Specifically, we estimate the linear probability model:

$$y_i = \alpha_0 + X_i\beta + \theta post\_reform_i + \lambda_1 quarter_i + \lambda_2 quarter_i^2 + \varepsilon_i.$$

In this model, *y* is a dummy variable that equals 1 if the individual is working in quarter 8 after injury and 0 otherwise; *X* is a vector of characteristics of the injured worker; *post_reform* is a dummy variable that equals 1 if the worker was injured after the reforms and 0 otherwise; and *quarter* is the quarter of injury.[1]

The characteristics of workers include age at the date of injury, the severity of the injury, preinjury wages, and the average fraction of uninjured control workers who are working. A natural measure of injury severity is the actual disability rating in the DEU. Given the changes that we know are occurring over this period, as described in Chapter Four, we adopt an alternative measure. We create a series of dummy variables indicating the quintiles of disability ratings within a year and use these dummy variables to capture severity (so, for example, the top dummy variable indicates that the injury was rated in the top quintile of injuries in the year).

An alternative specification is used comparing the outcomes of an injury type we think was especially affected by the reforms to a set of injuries that we think should have been largely unaffected. The "treated" workers are those with back injuries, while the "untreated" control group is comprised of workers with impaired vision, impaired hearing, lung disease, heart disease, psychiatric disabilities, or post-traumatic head syndrome.

Two key assumptions of this approach are that the quadratic term for quarter of injury captures the relevant time trends and that the dummy variable for postreform captures the discrete impact of the reform. Our experiments with other specifications and other periods of postinjury employment as the dependent variable did not yield qualitatively different results. Because we are using a linear probability model, we estimate heteroskedasticity-consistent "robust" standard errors.

---

[1] To be clear, the quarter of injury is sequential, so the first quarter of injury is quarter 1 in year 2000, while the eighth quarter is quarter 2 in 2001. We have 28 different quarters of injury in our data.

Table A.1 presents the full regression results. The first four columns report results for all workers, while the next six columns report results for firefighters only. For both occupation groups, we report results for all injuries, back injuries, shoulder injuries, and knee injuries. For firefighters, we report results for heart disease and, for the difference-in-differences specification, comparing treated back injuries to untreated injuries.

As described in the text, the reform variables are statistically insignificant in all specifications except for the all-workers, all-injuries specifications. The other variables perform as we would expect. Workers whose controls are more likely to be working in the eighth quarter after injury are more likely themselves to be working. Higher-wage workers are also more likely to be working. Workers with more severe injuries, as measured by disability rating quartile, are less likely to be working. Older workers are also less likely to be working.

Table A.1
Multivariate Regression Results

Result	All Occupations				Firefighters					
	All Injuries	Back Injuries	Shoulder Injuries	Knee Injuries	All Injuries	Back Injuries	Shoulder Injuries	Knee Injuries	Heart Disease	Difference in Differences
Dependent variable: working in quarter 8 after injury										
Postreform	−0.027	−0.034	−0.046	−0.018	0.017	0.017	0.026	0.034	−0.150	0.087
	(0.010)*	(0.022)	(0.034)	(0.023)	(0.027)	(0.053)	(0.068)	(0.044)	(0.200)	(0.078)
Treated × post										−0.085
										(0.067)
Untreated										−0.124
										(0.034)*
Control working	0.204	0.187	0.296	0.250	0.359	0.237	0.306	0.565	0.299	0.316
	(0.010)*	(0.020)*	(0.040)*	(0.031)*	(0.040)*	(0.090)*	(0.124)*	(0.091)*	(0.243)	(0.075)*
Preinjury wage	0.010	0.012	0.008	0.008	0.004	0.007	0.001	0.004	−0.001	0.007
	(0.000)*	(0.001)*	(0.001)*	(0.001)*	(0.001)*	(0.001)*	(0.002)	(0.001)*	(0.006)	(0.001)*
Quarter of injury	−14.030	−16.690	−33.718	3.411	−9.147	−23.323	−36.649	26.396	−53.533	−27.730
	(3.027)*	(7.154)*	(10.442)*	(7.153)	(8.656)	(16.934)	(19.222)*	(14.314)*	(53.133)	(15.658)*
Quarter of injury squared	0.004	0.004	0.008	−0.001	0.002	0.006	0.009	−0.007	0.013	0.007
	(0.001)*	(0.002)*	(0.003)*	(0.002)	(0.002)	(0.004)	(0.005)*	(0.004)*	(0.013)	(0.004)*
Severity quintile (bottom quintile omitted)										
2nd	−0.051	−0.052	−0.092	−0.003	−0.018	−0.038	−0.084	−0.011	−0.526	0.010
	(0.006)*	(0.012)*	(0.017)*	(0.012)	(0.014)	(0.022)*	(0.038)*	(0.024)	(0.175)*	(0.023)
3rd	−0.131	−0.137	−0.195	−0.094	−0.107	−0.097	−0.197	−0.084	−0.646	−0.067
	(0.007)*	(0.013)*	(0.022)*	(0.015)*	(0.018)*	(0.030)*	(0.060)*	(0.034)*	(0.161)*	(0.029)*

Table A.1—Continued

	All Occupations				Firefighters					
Result	All Injuries	Back Injuries	Shoulder Injuries	Knee Injuries	All Injuries	Back Injuries	Shoulder Injuries	Knee Injuries	Heart Disease	Difference in Differences
4th	−0.225	−0.224	−0.255	−0.226	−0.182	−0.207	−0.248	−0.215	−0.512	−0.144
	(0.007)*	(0.013)*	(0.032)*	(0.020)*	(0.023)*	(0.037)*	(0.098)*	(0.056)*	(0.181)*	(0.036)*
5th	−0.331	−0.345	−0.221	−0.310	−0.331	−0.413	−0.191	−0.221	−0.573	−0.295
	(0.008)*	(0.015)*	(0.057)*	(0.025)*	(0.025)*	(0.048)*	(0.200)	(0.083)*	(0.142)*	(0.042)*
Age category (25–34 omitted)										
35–44	0.012	−0.003	0.034	0.029	0.038	0.046	−0.022	−0.018	0.000	0.043
	(0.006)*	(0.011)	(0.021)	(0.014)*	(0.016)*	(0.029)	(0.032)	(0.024)	(0.000)	(0.029)
45–54	−0.018	−0.034	0.006	0.003	−0.070	−0.066	−0.081	−0.105	−0.274	−0.097
	(0.006)*	(0.012)*	(0.022)	(0.015)	(0.018)*	(0.033)*	(0.034)*	(0.029)*	(0.079)*	(0.033)*
55 and over	−0.130	−0.147	−0.103	−0.129	−0.350	−0.331	−0.474	−0.462	−0.599	−0.381
	(0.008)*	(0.018)*	(0.030)*	(0.022)*	(0.026)*	(0.057)*	(0.076)*	(0.059)*	(0.096)*	(0.047)*
Observations	42,191	10,075	3,074	5,350	4,318	1,055	454	802	108	1,365
R-squared	0.26	0.27	0.24	0.25	0.30	0.28	0.27	0.28	0.25	0.26

NOTE: Table reports the estimates from a linear probability model of the impact of the workers' compensation reforms and other variables on the likelihood of return to work, by occupation and injury type. The first four columns report the results for all occupations for different combinations of injury. The final six columns report the results with the sample restricted to firefighters. Treated injuries in the final column are back injuries, while the untreated injuries include impaired vision, impaired hearing, lung disease, heart disease, psychiatric disabilities, and post-traumatic head syndrome. For the all-occupations regressions, a set of occupation dummies is included, while, for the all-injuries regressions, a set of injury-type dummies is included. Robust standard errors are reported in parentheses. A * represents statistical significance at the 10% level or better.

Bibliography

Akpala, C. O., A. P. Curran, and J. Simpson, "Physiotherapy in General Practice: Patterns of Utilisation," *Public Health*, Vol. 102, No. 3, May 1988, pp. 263–268.

AMA Guides—*See* Cocchiarella and Andersson (2001).

Assendelft, Willem J. J., Sally C. Morton, Emily I. Yu, Marika J. Suttorp, and Paul G. Shekelle, "Spinal Manipulative Therapy for Low Back Pain: A Meta-Analysis of Effectiveness Relative to Other Therapies," *Annals of Internal Medicine*, Vol. 138, No. 11, June 3, 2003, pp. 871–881.

Baldwin, Marjorie L., Pierre Côté, John W. Frank, and William G. Johnson, "Cost-Effectiveness Studies of Medical and Chiropractic Care for Occupational Low Back Pain: A Critical Review of the Literature," *Spine*, Vol. 1, No. 2, March 2001, pp. 138–147.

California Commission on Health and Safety and Workers' Compensation, *CHSWC 2006 Annual Report*, State of California Labor and Workforce Development Agency, Department of Industrial Relations, December 2006. As of May 25, 2010:
http://www.dir.ca.gov/CHSWC/Reports/AnnualReport2006.pdf

———, *CHSWC 2007 Annual Report*, State of California Labor and Workforce Development Agency, Department of Industrial Relations, December 2007. As of May 25, 2010:
http://www.dir.ca.gov/CHSWC/Reports/AnnualReport2007.pdf

California Education Code, Section 1294.

———, Section 44984.

California Labor Code, Section 4062.9.

———, Section 4463.

———, Section 4604.5.

———, Section 4610.

———, Section 4660.

———, Section 4663.

———, Section 4664.

———, Section 4750.

———, Section 4850.

———, Section 4859.

California Senate Bill 228, Administrative Reorganization, chaptered October 1, 2003. As of May 26, 2010:
http://info.sen.ca.gov/cgi-bin/postquery?bill_number=sb_228&sess=0304&house=B&site=

California Senate Bill 899, Workers' Compensation, chaptered April 19, 2004. As of May 26, 2010:
http://info.sen.ca.gov/cgi-bin/postquery?bill_number=sb_899&sess=0304&house=B&site=sen

Carey, Timothy S., Janet K. Freburger, George M. Holmes, Liana Castel, Jane Darter, Robert Agans, William Kalsbeek, and Anne Jackman, "A Long Way to Go: Practice Patterns and Evidence in Chronic Low Back Pain Care," *Spine*, Vol. 34, No. 7, April 1, 2009, pp. 718–724.

Carey, Timothy S., Joanne Garett, Anne Jackman, Curtis McLaughlin, John Fryer, and Douglas R. Smucker, "The Outcomes and Costs of Care for Acute Low Back Pain Among Patients Seen by Primary Care Practitioners, Chiropractors, and Orthopedic Surgeons," *New England Journal of Medicine*, Vol. 333, No. 14, October 5, 1995, pp. 913–917.

Chau, N., P. Wild, D. Dehaene, L. Benamghar, J. M. Mur, and C. Touron, "Roles of Age, Length of Service and Job in Work-Related Injury: A Prospective Study of 466,120 Person-Years in Railway Workers," *Occupational and Environmental Medicine*, Vol. 67, 2010, pp. 147–153.

Cherkin, Daniel C., Richard A. Deyo, Michele Battié, Janet Street, and William Barlow, "A Comparison of Physical Therapy, Chiropractic Manipulation, and Provision of an Educational Booklet for the Treatment of Patients with Low Back Pain," *New England Journal of Medicine*, Vol. 339, No. 15, October 8, 1998, pp. 1021–1029.

Cherkin, Daniel C., Karen J. Sherman, Richard A. Deyo, and Paul G. Shekelle, "A Review of the Evidence for the Effectiveness, Safety, and Cost of Acupuncture, Massage Therapy, and Spinal Manipulation for Back Pain," *Annals of Internal Medicine*, Vol. 138, No. 11, June 3, 2002, pp. 898–906.

CHSWC—*See* California Commission on Health and Safety and Workers' Compensation.

Clarke, Cindy, and Mark J. Zak, *Fatalities to Law Enforcement Officers and Firefighters, 1992–97*, Emmitsburg, Md.: National Emergency Training Center, 1999. As of May 25, 2010:
http://www.bls.gov/opub/cwc/archive/summer1999art1.pdf

Cocchiarella, Linda, and Gunnar Andersson, eds., *Guides to the Evaluation of Permanent Impairment*, 5th ed., Chicago, Ill.: American Medical Association, 2001.

Deyle, Gail D., Nancy E. Henderson, Robert L. Matekel, Michael G. Ryder, Matthew B. Garber, and Stephen C. Allison, "Effectiveness of Manual Physical Therapy and Exercise in Osteoarthritis of the Knee: A Randomized, Controlled Trial," *Annals of Internal Medicine*, Vol. 132, No. 3, February 1, 2000, pp. 173–181.

Ehrmann-Feldman, D., M. Rossignol, L. Abenhaim, and D. Gobeille, "Physician Referral to Physical Therapy in a Cohort of Workers Compensated for Low Back Pain," *Physical Therapy*, Vol. 76, No. 2, February 1996, pp. 150–156, discussion pp. 156–157.

Eisenberg, David M., Ronald C. Kessler, Cindy Foster, Frances E. Norlock, David R. Calkins, and Thomas L. Delbanco, "Unconventional Medicine in the United States: Prevalence, Costs, and Patterns of Use," *New England Journal of Medicine*, Vol. 328, No. 4, January 28, 1993, pp. 246–252.

Eisenberg, David M., Diana E. Post, Roger B. Davis, Maureen T. Connelly, Anna T. R. Legedza, Andrea L. Hrbek, Lisa A. Prosser, Julie E. Buring, Thomas S. Inui, and Daniel C. Cherkin, "Addition of Choice of Complementary Therapies to Usual Care for Acute Low Back Pain: A Randomized Controlled Trial," *Spine*, Vol. 32, No. 2, January 15, 2007, pp. 151–158.

Frank, John W., Mickey S. Kerr, Ann-Sylvia Brooker, Suzanne E. DeMaio, Andreas Maetzel, Harry S. Shannon, Terry J. Sullivan, Robert W. Norman, and Richard P. Wells, "Disability Resulting from Occupational Low Back Pain, Part I: What Do We Know About Primary Prevention? A Review of the Scientific Evidence on Prevention Before Disability Begins," *Spine*, Vol. 21, No. 24, December 15, 1996, pp. 2908–2917.

Goldby, Lucy Jane, Ann P. Moore, Jo Doust, and Marion E. Trew, "A Randomized Controlled Trial Investigating the Efficiency of Musculoskeletal Physiotherapy on Chronic Low Back Disorder," *Spine*, Vol. 31, No. 10, May 1, 2006, pp. 1083–1093.

Guidotti, Tee L., "Apportionment in Asbestos-Related Disease for Purposes of Compensation," *Industrial Health*, Vol. 40, No. 4, October 2002, pp. 295–311.

———, "The Big Bang? An Eventful Year in Workers' Compensation," Annual Review of Public Health, Vol. 27, 2006, pp. 153–166.

Haas, M., B. Goldberg, M. Aickin, B. Ganger, and M. Attwood, "A Practice-Based Study of Patients with Acute and Chronic Low Back Pain Attending Primary Care and Chiropractic Physicians: Two-Week to 48-Month Follow-Up," *Journal of Manipulative and Physiological Therapeutics*, Vol. 27, No. 3, March–April 2004, pp. 160–169.

Hashemi, L., B. S. Webster, E. A. Clancy, and T. K. Courtney, "Length of Disability and Cost of Work-Related Musculoskeletal Disorders of the Upper Extremity," *Journal of Occupational and Environmental Medicine*, Vol. 40, No. 3, March 1998, pp. 261–269.

Heckman, James J., and V. Joseph Hotz, "Choosing Among Alternative Nonexperimental Methods for Estimating the Impact of Social Programs: The Case of Manpower Training," *Journal of the American Statistical Association*, Vol. 84, No. 408, December 1989, pp. 862–874.

Holland, Paul W., "Statistics and Causal Inference," *Journal of the American Statistical Association*, Vol. 81, No. 396, December 1986, pp. 945–960.

Hoving, Jan Lucas, Bart W. Koes, Henrica C. W. de Vet, Danielle A. W. M. van der Windt, Williem J. J. Assendelft, Henk van Mameren, Walter L. J. M. Devillé, Jan J. M. Pool, Rob J. P. M. Scholten, and Lex M. Bouter, "Manual Therapy, Physical Therapy, or Continued Care by a General Practitioner for Patients with Neck Pain: A Randomized, Controlled Trial," *Annals of Internal Medicine*, Vol. 136, No. 10, May 21, 2002, pp. 713–722.

Hurwitz, Eric, Ian D. Coulter, Alan H. Adams, Barbara Genovese, and Paul G. Shekelle, "Use of Chiropractic Services from 1985 Through 1991 in the United States and Canada," *American Journal of Public Health*, Vol. 88, No. 5, May 1998, pp. 771–776. Reprint available as of May 25, 2010: http://www.rand.org/pubs/reprints/RP827/

Hurwitz, Eric L., Hal Morgenstern, Philip Harber, Gerald F. Kominski, Thomas R. Belin, Fei Yu, and Alan H. Adams, "A Randomized Trial of Medical Care with and Without Physical Therapy and Chiropractic Care with and Without Physical Modalities for Patients with Low Back Pain: 6-Month Follow-Up Outcomes from the UCLA Low Back Pain Study," *Spine*, Vol. 27, No. 20, October 15, 2002, pp. 2193–2204.

Hurwitz, Eric L., Hal Morgenstern, Gerald F. Kominski, Fei Yu, and A. H. Adams, "A Randomized Trial of Chiropractic Manipulation and Mobilization for Patients with Neck Pain: Clinical Outcomes from the UCLA Neck-Pain Study," *American Journal of Public Health*, Vol. 92, No. 10, October 2002, pp. 1634–1641.

Hurwitz, Eric L., Hal Morgenstern, Gerald F. Kominski, Fei Yu, and Lu-May Chiang, "A Randomized Trial of Chiropractic and Medical Care for Patients with Low Back Pain: Eighteen-Month Follow-Up Outcomes from the UCLA Low Back Pain Study," *Spine*, Vol. 31, No. 6, March 15, 2006, pp. 611–621.

IAFF—*See* International Association of Fire Fighters.

International Association of Fire Fighters, *2000 Death and Injury Survey*, Washington, D.C., c. 2000. As of May 25, 2010: http://www.iaff.org/hs/PDF/2000%20D&I.pdf

Jette, Alan M., Kevin Smith, Stephen M. Haley, and Kenneth D. Davis, "Physical Therapy Episodes of Care for Patients with Low Back Pain," *Physical Therapy*, Vol. 74, No. 2, February 1994, pp. 101–110.

Johnson, M. R., M. K. Schultz, and A. C. Ferguson, "A Comparison of Chiropractic, Medical and Osteopathic Care for Work-Related Sprains and Strains," *Journal of Manipulative and Physiological Therapeutics*, Vol. 12, No. 5, October 1989, pp. 335–344.

Johnson, William G., Marjorie L. Baldwin, and Richard J. Butler, "The Costs and Outcomes of Chiropractic and Physician Care for Workers' Compensation Back Claims," *Journal of Risk and Insurance*, Vol. 66, No. 2, June 1999, pp. 185–205.

Koes, B. W., L. M. Bouter, H. van Mameren, A. H. Esserts, G. M. Verstegen, D. M. Hofhuizen, J. P. Houben, and P. G. Knipschild, "The Effectiveness of Manual Therapy, Physiotherapy, and Treatment by the General Practitioner for Nonspecific Back and Neck Complaints: A Randomized Clinical Trial," *Spine*, Vol. 17, No. 1, January 1992, pp. 28–35.

LaLonde, Robert J., "Evaluating the Econometric Evaluations of Training Programs with Experimental Data," *American Economic Review*, Vol. 76, No. 4, September 1986, pp. 604–620.

LaTourrette, Tom, David S. Loughran, and Seth A. Seabury, *Occupational Safety and Health for Public Safety Employees: Assessing the Evidence and the Implications for Public Policy*, Santa Monica, Calif.: RAND Corporation, MG-792-CHSWC/NIOSH, 2008. As of May 25, 2010: http://www.rand.org/pubs/monographs/MG792/

Lipscomb, Hester J., John M. Dement, Barbara Silverstein, Kristen L. Kucera, and Wilfrid Cameron, "Health Care Utilization for Musculoskeletal Back Disorders, Washington State Union Carpenters, 1989–2003," *Journal of Occupational and Environmental Medicine*, Vol. 51, No. 5, May 2009, pp. 604–611.

Luijsterburg, Pim A. J., Leida M. Lamers, Arianne P. Verhagen, Raymond W. J. G. Ostelo, Hans J. M. M. van den Hoogen, Wilco C. Peul, Cees J. J. Avezaat, and Bart Koes, "Cost-Effectiveness of Physical Therapy and General Practitioner Care for Sciatica," *Spine*, Vol. 32, No. 18, August 15, 2007, pp. 1942–1948.

Meade, T. W., S. Dyer, W. Browne, J. Townsend, and A. O. Frank, "Low Back Pain of Mechanical Origin: Randomised Comparison of Chiropractic and Hospital Outpatient Treatment," *British Medical Journal*, Vol. 300, June 2, 1990, pp. 1431–1437.

Melhorn, J. Mark, Larry Wilkinson, and James D. Riggs, "Management of Musculoskeletal Pain in the Workplace," *Journal of Occupational and Environmental Medicine*, Vol. 43, No. 2, February 2001, pp. 83–93.

Metz, R. Douglas, Craig F. Nelson, Thomas LaBrot, and Kenneth R. Pelletier, "Chiropractic Care: Is It Substitution Care or Add-On Care in Corporate Medical Plans?" *Journal of Occupational and Environmental Medicine*, Vol. 46, No. 8, August 2004, pp. 847–855.

Meyer, Bruce D., W. Kip Viscusi, and David L. Durbin, "Workers' Compensation and Injury Duration: Evidence from a Natural Experiment," *American Economic Review*, Vol. 85, No. 3, June 1995, pp. 322–340.

Mielenz, Thelma J., Timothy S. Carey, Daniel A. Dyrek, Bette A. Harris, JoAnn M. Garrett, and Jane D. Darter, "Physical Therapy Utilization by Patients with Acute Low Back Pain," *Physical Therapy*, Vol. 77, No. 10, October 1997, pp. 1040–1051.

Murt, H., P. E. Parsons, W. R. Harlan, J. W. Thomas, J. M. Lepkowski, K. E. Guire, S. Berki, and J. R. Landis, "Disability, Utilization, and Costs Associated with Musculoskeletal Conditions," *National Medical Care Utilization and Expenditures Survey*, Series C, No. 5, September 1986, pp. 1–64.

Neuhauser, Frank, "Analysis of Ratings Under the New PD Schedule, Through June 30, 2007," memorandum to Commission on Health and Safety and Workers' Compensation, August 8, 2007.

Niemistö, Leena, Pekka Rissanen, Seppo Sarna, Tiina Lahtinen-Suopanki, Karl-August Lindgren, and Heikki Hurri, "Cost-Effectiveness of Combined Manipulation, Stabilizing Exercises, and Physician Consultation Compared to Physician Consultation Alone for Chronic Low Back Pain: A Prospective Randomized Trial with 2-Year Follow-Up," *Spine*, Vol. 30, No. 10, May 15, 2005, pp. 1109–1115.

Nuckols, Teryl K., Barbara O. Wynn, Yee-Wei Lim, Rebecca Shaw, Soeren Mattke, Thomas Wickizer, Philip Harber, Peggy Wallace, Steven M. Asch, Catherine MacLean, and Rena Hasenfeld Garland, *Evaluating Medical Treatment Guideline Sets for Injured Workers in California*, Santa Monica, Calif.: RAND Corporation, MG-400-ICJ, 2005. As of June 4, 2010:
http://www.rand.org/pubs/monographs/MG400/

Pengel, Liset H. M., Kathryn M. Refshauge, Christopher G. Maher, Michael K. Nicholas, Robert D. Herbert, and Peter McNair, "Physiotherapist-Directed Exercise, Advice, or Both for Subacute Low Back Pain: A Randomized Trial," *Annals of Internal Medicine*, Vol. 146, No. 11, June 5, 2007, pp. 787–796.

Peterson, Mark A., Robert T. Reville, Rachel Kaganoff Stern, and Peter S. Barth, *Compensating Permanent Workplace Injuries: A Study of the California System*, Santa Monica, Calif.: RAND Corporation, MR-920-ICJ, 1998. As of May 25, 2010:
http://www.rand.org/pubs/monograph_reports/MR920/

Punnett, Laura, and David H. Wegman, "Work-Related Musculoskeletal Disorders: The Epidemiological Evidence and the Debate," *Journal of Electromyography and Kinesiology*, Vol. 14, No. 1, February 2004, pp. 13–23.

Reville, Robert T., Jay Bhattacharya, and Lauren R. Sager Weinstein, "New Methods and Data Sources for Measuring Economic Consequences of Workplace Injuries," *American Journal of Industrial Medicine*, Vol. 40, No. 4, October 2001, pp. 452–463. Reprint available as of May 15, 2010:
http://www.rand.org/pubs/reprints/RP972/

Reville, Robert T., Leslie I. Boden, Jeff E. Biddle, and Christopher Mardesich, *An Evaluation of New Mexico Workers' Compensation Permanent Partial Disability and Return to Work*, Santa Monica, Calif.: RAND Corporation, MR-1414-ICJ, 2001. As of June 4, 2010:
http://www.rand.org/pubs/monograph_reports/MR1414/

Reville, Robert T., and Robert F. Schoeni, *Disability from Injuries at Work: The Effects on Earnings and Employment*, Santa Monica, Calif.: RAND Corporation, DRU-2554, 2001. As of May 15, 2010:
http://www.rand.org/pubs/drafts/DRU2554/

Reville, Robert T., Robert F. Schoeni, and Craig Martin, *Trends in Earnings Loss from Disabling Workplace Injuries in California: The Role of Economic Conditions*, Santa Monica, Calif.: RAND Corporation, MR-1457-ICJ, 2002. As of June 4, 2010:
http://www.rand.org/pubs/monograph_reports/MR1457/

Reville, Robert T., Seth A. Seabury, Frank W. Neuhauser, John F. Burton Jr., and Michael D. Greenburg, *An Evaluation of California's Permanent Disability Rating System*, Santa Monica, Calif.: RAND Corporation, MG-258-ICJ, 2005. As of May 15, 2010:
http://www.rand.org/pubs/monographs/MG258/

SB—*See* California Senate Bill.

Seabury, Seth A., Robert T. Reville, and Frank Neuhauser, "Physician Shopping in Workers' Compensation: Evidence from California," *Journal of Empirical Legal Studies*, Vol. 3, No. 1, March 2006, pp. 47–77.

Shekelle, P. G., and R. H. Brook, "A Community-Based Study of the Use of Chiropractic Services," *American Journal of Public Health*, Vol. 81, No. 4, April 1991, pp. 439–442.

Shekelle, Paul G., Martin Markovich, and Rachel Louie, "Comparing the Costs Between Provider Types of Episodes of Back Pain Care," *Spine*, Vol. 20, No. 2, January 15, 1995a, pp. 221–227.

———, "An Epidemiologic Study of Episodes of Back Pain Care," *Spine*, Vol. 20, No. 15, August 1995b, pp. 1668–1673.

Solomon, Daniel H., David W. Bates, Richard S. Panush, and Jeffrey N. Katz, "Costs, Outcomes, and Patient Satisfaction by Provider Type for Patients with Rheumatic and Musculoskeletal Conditions: A Critical Review of the Literature and Proposed Methodologic Standards," *Annals of Internal Medicine*, Vol. 127, No. 1, July 1, 1997, pp. 52–60.

Swedlow, A., *The Utilization and Cost of Physical Therapy and Chiropractic Manipulation in California Workers' Compensation Following Implementation of Mandatory Utilization Review and 24-Visit Caps*, Oakland, Calif.: California Workers' Compensation Institute, 2005.

Torstensen, T. A., A. E. Ljunggren, H. D. Meen, E. Odland, P. Mowinckel, and S. Geijerstam, "Efficiency and Costs of Medical Exercise Therapy, Conventional Physiotherapy, and Self-Exercise in Patients with Chronic Low Back Pain: A Pragmatic, Randomized, Single-Blinded, Controlled Trial with 1-Year Follow-Up," *Spine*, Vol. 23, No. 23, December 1, 1998, pp. 2616–2624.

Tsauo, Jau-Yih, Huey-Wen Liang, Yuh Jang, and Chung-Li Du, "Physical Therapy Utilization in Subjects with Work-Related Musculoskeletal Disorders: Taiwan Experience," *Journal of Occupational Rehabilitation*, Vol. 19, No. 1, March 2009, pp. 106–112.

Walker, M. J., R. E. Boyles, B. A. Young, J. B. Strunce, M. B. Garber, J. M. Whitman, G. Deyle, and R. S. Wainner, "The Effectiveness of Manual Physical Therapy and Exercise for Mechanical Neck Pain: A Randomized Clinical Trial," *Spine*, Vol. 33, No. 22, October 15, 2008, pp. 2371–2378.

Walton, Surrey M., Karen M. Conrad, Sylvia E. Furner, and Daniel G. Samo, "Cause, Type, and Workers' Compensation Costs of Injury to Fire Fighters," *American Journal of Industrial Medicine*, Vol. 43, No. 4, April 2003, pp. 454–458.

Wasiak, Radoslaw, and Eileen McNeely, "Utilization and Costs of Chiropractic Care for Work-Related Low Back Injuries: Do Payment Policies Make a Difference?" *Spine*, Vol. 6, No. 2, March–April 2006, pp. 146–153.

Wasiak, R., J. Kim, and G. S. Pransky, "The Association Between Timing and Duration of Chiropractic Care in Work-Related Low Back Pain and Work-Disability Outcomes," *Journal of Occupational and Environmental Medicine*, Vol. 49, No. 10, October 2007, pp. 1124–1134.

Zigenfus, G. C., J. Yin, G. M. Giang, and W. T. Fogarty, "Effectiveness of Early Physical Therapy in the Treatment of Acute Low Back Musculoskeletal Disorders," *Journal of Occupational and Environmental Medicine*, Vol. 42, No. 1, January 2000, pp. 35–39.